TRAIN YOUR
BRAIN TO
GET RICH

TRAIN YOUR BRAIN TO GET RICH

THE SIMPLE PROGRAM THAT PRIMES YOUR GRAY CELLS FOR

WEALTH, PROSPERITY, AND FINANCIAL SECURITY

Teresa Aubele, PhD, Doug Freeman, JD, LLM,
Lee Hausner, PhD, and Susan Reynolds

Avon, Massachusetts

Published by
Adams Media, a division of F+W Media, Inc.
57 Littlefield Street, Avon, MA 02322. U.S.A.
www.adamsmedia.com

Contains material adapted and abridged from:
365 Ways to Boost Your Metabolism by Rachel Laferriere, MS, RD, copyright © 2010 by F+W
Media, Inc., ISBN 10: 1-4405-0213-7, ISBN 13: 978-1-4405-0213-2.

ISBN 10: 1-4405-2808-X
ISBN 13: 978-1-4405-2808-8
eISBN 10: 1-4405-2909-4
eISBN 13: 978-1-4405-2909-2

Printed in the United States of America.

10 9 8 7 6 5 4 3 2 1

Library of Congress Cataloging-in-Publication Data
is available from the publisher.

The information in this book should not be used for diagnosing or treating any health problem. You should always consult a trained medical professional before starting a health program, taking any form of medication, or embarking on any fitness program. The author and publisher disclaim any liability arising directly or indirectly from the use of this book.

This publication is designed to provide accurate and authoritative information with regard to the subject matter covered. It is sold with the understanding that the publisher is not engaged in rendering legal, accounting, or other professional advice. If legal advice or other expert assistance is required, the services of a competent professional person should be sought.
—From a *Declaration of Principles* jointly adopted by a Committee of the American Bar Association and a Committee of Publishers and Associations

Many of the designations used by manufacturers and sellers to distinguish their product are claimed as trademarks. Where those designations appear in this book and Adams Media was aware of a trademark claim, the designations have been printed with initial capital letters.

This book is available at quantity discounts for bulk purchases.
For information, please call 1-800-289-0963.

CONTENTS

INTRODUCTION

"Think and grow rich."

—Napoleon Hill

Napoleon Hill was right—everyone can think themselves rich, if they only had a rich-thinking brain. If you're someone who remembers struggling in math classes or who dismisses the notion of paying close attention to your finances because you "don't have a head for numbers," *Train Your Brain to Get Rich* is just the book you need to give you the knowledge and confidence to develop a successful wealth creation program.

Your brain is an extraordinary organ, but until recently its inner workings remained somewhat of a mystery. It was commonly believed that once the brain had developed, the only change occurring was the deterioration accompanying the aging process. However, today, the explosion in the field of brain research has unlocked the inner workings of this master organ and the results demonstrate exciting news about how the brain continually evolves and what role our thoughts can have in creating a rich-thinking brain.

Train Your Brain to Get Rich integrates recent breakthroughs in neuroscience with wealth creation to help you learn how to:

- *Understand the inner workings of your brain*—how it works for you and against you in your quest for wealth.
- *Make more money*, by strengthening the thoughtful, analytic part of your brain in order to identify the best business and investment opportunities.

- *Invest more wisely,* by short-circuiting unproductive habits that facilitate faulty reasoning.
- *Rebound from financial setbacks,* without getting trapped by your brain's fight-or-flight response.
- *Budget to acquire investment capital,* by maximizing your brain skills when setting goals.
- *Achieve desired financial goals,* by strengthening the brain's ability to ignore distractions and remain purposeful and focused.

All those tools and more will help you begin your training process and take control of your finances. If you want to use your brain's rich resources to create wealth, don't waste another minute . . . your fortune awaits!

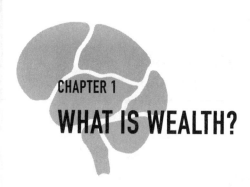

CHAPTER 1

WHAT IS WEALTH?

Principle: We all want wealth—who wouldn't?—but you can't know what form of wealth you want until you know what you value.

Whether you are aware of it or not, much of what you know about money, your thoughts involving money, and the way you make financial decisions have already been ingrained in your brain. This knowledge resulted from what you saw your parents doing, or from listening to what they taught you, or from observing other people. Perhaps you've consciously taken a different route with earning, spending, and investing money, but that doesn't mean that your brain has entirely caught up with your plans. To train your brain to get rich, you first need to know what's stored in your memory and how the way your brain understands money could be affecting you more than you think.

This chapter, in particular, will help you shine a light in the corners of your mind/brain to see how much it knows (or doesn't know!) about wealth creation. Here, we'll discuss the concept of money—as your brain understands and relates to it—and ideas you may have about money that you might not even know are affecting your wealth creation. But before we start to learn about your brain, and the way it thinks about money, let's take a few minutes to assess your need to train your brain to get rich.

WHY YOU NEED TO TRAIN YOUR BRAIN TO GET RICH

Unless you're already a self-made millionaire, it's highly likely that you're not using your brain to its fullest capacity in wealth creation. Let's begin by assessing where you are on the wealth creation scale.

The *How I'm Doing on the Money Front* Quiz

1. **When it came to money, my parents:**
   - **A.** taught me how to manage money and be frugal.
   - **B.** generally set a good example but didn't talk about money much.
   - **C.** groused about never having enough, but didn't do anything to change it.
   - **D.** didn't have a clue and were always broke.

2. **When it comes to a career, I:**
   - **A.** set my sights early on to enter a high-paying profession.
   - **B.** didn't give it enough thought and now regret my choice.
   - **C.** don't have a career; I have a job (that I don't particularly like).
   - **D.** am not even sure what a career would look like.

3. **When it comes to the amount of money I make, I am:**
   - **A.** doing okay, but always aspiring to make more.
   - **B.** well below where I hoped I'd be at this point in my life.
   - **C.** stuck at a certain level and always passed over for promotions.
   - **D.** barely above water, very unhappy, and don't see a lot of options.

4. **When it comes to making investments, I:**
   - **A.** have a long-term plan in place that I review every five years.
   - **B.** put money in my IRA every year, but it's all cash.

C. invested in a house, but have no other investments.

D. don't have enough money to invest in anything.

5. **When I have to make a big financial decision, I:**

   A. research and carefully weigh all my options before making decisions.

   B. hire an investment counselor and do whatever he recommends.

   C. put it off for months until I'm forced to deal with it.

   D. no money = no financial decisions.

6. **I would describe my financial savvy as:**

   A. substantial, but there's a lot I could learn.

   B. fairly solid for everyday decisions, but lacking overall.

   C. very unsophisticated, about where I was in high school.

   D. Zero. Zilch. Nada.

7. **My savings account is:**

   A. one of my top priorities.

   B. building slowly, but not nearly as fast as I'd like it to grow.

   C. way below what it should be.

   D. nonexistent.

8. **When it comes to an "emergency plan," I:**

   A. have set aside three months' living expenses in an untouchable savings account.

   B. have about $1,000 in my savings that I don't tap—unless I have to.

   C. don't have one because there's never enough money for savings.

   D. my whole life is an emergency.

9. **To stay current about financial matters and markets, I:**
    A. read financial magazines, talk with my broker, and review financial reports.
    B. watch the financial shows on television, read the Wall Street Journal occasionally.
    C. don't pay much attention, unless it directly affects me.
    D. have no reason to pay attention because I don't have any extra money to invest.

Answer Key

If you chose mostly As, you have a solid financial base to build on, but could use a booster shot to take you to the next level. Your brain is ripe for training and will respond positively to the suggestions offered throughout this book. In no time, you'll be creating greater wealth—and happiness.

If you chose mostly Bs, your financial base is somewhat lacking, but salvageable. With a little work, you can bolster your financial knowledge, learn ways to make your brain work harder for you, and increase your wealth substantially. This book is chock full of ideas for you—and you don't have be a math whiz to benefit greatly.

If you chose mostly Cs, there's a lot of work to be done. Still, you are eager to feel more confident and to discover ways that you can move up the ladder, both career-wise and money-wise. With a little focused tweaking, your brain will soon be lighting the way to wealth.

If you chose mostly Ds, your brain has a lot of catch-up work to be done. You simply weren't given the knowledge you needed to create wealth, but it's not too late. Changing your approach to wealth creation won't be nearly as hard, or discouraging, as you might fear. You can get your brain up and running in no time.

WHY YOUR BRAIN IS PLAYING CATCH-UP

Thanks to millions of years of evolution, we are highly intelligent biological organisms, but when it comes to making financial decisions, we can be unduly influenced by ancient brain skills. Our evolution not only drives the decisions we make when we face similar situations to those of our ancestors, but also those that our ancient ancestors could never have envisioned. Until very recent history—in evolutionary terms—humans were hunter-gatherers, living in small nomadic bands, seeking mates, procreating, finding shelter, foraging for food, and pursuing prey they could eat while avoiding predators who wanted to eat them.

Humans are not the only animals that make tools, show insight, or plan for the future. But no other species can match our phenomenal ability to forecast and extrapolate, to observe correlations, and to infer cause from effect. Our brains are at least three times the size of gorilla or chimpanzee brains, but in the 200,000 years since *Homo sapiens* evolved, the human brain has remained roughly the same size. Most of the "modern" areas of the human brain, such as our left prefrontal cortex (considered the CEO of our brains) developed largely during the Stone Age and haven't changed much since.

In financial realms, domesticated food crops and the first cities date back only 11,000 years, and the earliest known financial markets, trading in food crops and silver, sprang up in Mesopotamia around 2500 B.C. Formal stock and bond trading markets came to be a mere four centuries ago. All of which means that, when it comes to money, your brain has had a lot of catching up to do in a very short time.

Your Brain's Limitations

Your brain is a whiz at certain things: recognizing simple patterns or generating emotional responses in nanoseconds but lags behind on other tasks: recognizing and evaluating long-term financial or business trends, recognizing when patterns are truly random, or focusing on many things at one time. Your brain is also trained to respond to fear, and will assume some situations are dangerous even when they aren't. All of these abilities and instincts are challenged (and challenging to overcome!) when making financial decisions.

Luckily, we are at the forefront of new brain exploration, which is offering amazing insights into how the human brain works and how you can maximize your brain's capabilities. Thanks to breakthroughs in neuroscience, we all have the capability to understand a lot more about how this magnificently complex structure we call our brain operates and what we can do to enhance its development in all areas of our lives, including personal and financial well-being.

We've got a wealth of ideas and knowledge to speed you along your quest to get rich . . . but first you have to determine what wealth means to you!

WHAT DOES BEING RICH MEAN TO YOU?

Your immediate reaction might be that of a specific number in a bank account, but, in fact, your wealth is actually the sum total of four important capital accounts:

1. **Human Capital:** All the activities that enhance personal and interpersonal development.
2. **Intellectual Capital:** All the activities that expand your knowledge base.
3. **Financial Capital:** How you make, manage, preserve, and transfer money.
4. **Social Capital:** How you utilize your empathy to make the world a better place.

As we operate in a world where both material values and spiritual values are important, the goal to ultimate satisfaction is to find balance between these forces. Acknowledging that "being rich" encompasses many aspects of development broadens your perspective on the entire subject. As you work your way through this book, you will be able to understand how you can more effectively utilize the power of your brain to enhance all these capital accounts, thereby achieving "richness" in all aspects of your life.

WHY MONEY ITSELF DOESN'T MOTIVATE YOUR BRAIN

Money in itself doesn't satisfy a basic need for survival, like food, water, shelter, and sex. Money is just paper, after all; it's what money represents to us that has value. Money is therefore called a "secondary reinforcer" because, while it can be used to purchase a "primary" reward (food, water), it isn't a primary reward in and of itself. Actually, what you buy with your money might be a secondary reward, too! When using money, your train of thought can often go something like this:

Money (secondary reinforcer) → buy a yacht (secondary reinforcer) → attract a potential mate (secondary reinforcer) → fall in love (secondary reinforcer) → reproduce (primary reward).

Thus, money becomes more or less powerful based on your view of it and how you elect to use it. Unfortunately, your brain can have trouble with subjectivity. For example, if you have a huge dream peppered with lots of reinforcers, your brain may feel so overwhelmed that it will rely on emotion rather than logically deciding which reinforcer needs to take precedence. Getting to the heart of your desires and breaking down your dreams into smaller, more attainable goals will make it easier for your logical brain to help you deliver the goods.

What Price Happiness?

Your mother was right when she told you "money doesn't make you happy." Multiple studies have found that having money beyond a certain level (around $50,000 to $75,000 in annual income) in America doesn't vastly improve happiness levels. If someone is living at or below the poverty level, having enough annual income to move up the economic scale (even if only as far as the middle class) will make them happier, but mostly because it allows them to fulfill their basic needs, such as shelter and food, more easily. So what's your set point for wealth? Are you the type of person who "needs" at least $200,000 in annual income to feel wealthy? Or, would you be happy as a clam if you had $75,000 in annual income and had plenty of money and time for recreation and travel?

WHAT DOES THE TERM "WEALTH" MEAN TO YOU?

When a prominent financial expert spoke to a large class of graduating college seniors, she asked the largely female audience how they felt about the word "wealth." Nearly all of the young women—all of whom were very bright—either didn't relate to the word wealth or thought that wealth was something other people would achieve rather than them.

In digging a little further, the financial expert found that these same women related strongly to desires for financial security, becoming good at managing money, and achieving peace of mind.

While money in itself wouldn't motivate them, these other desires did. But because of their inability to connect the dots between money and their desires, they would very likely have difficulty acquiring wealth.

Defining exactly what wealth looks like to you—and what value you place on it—is an important component to the process of acquiring wealth.

Where Did You Get Your Ideas about Money?

Like the graduating women, each of us comes into adulthood bearing personal money scripts, conscious and unconscious ideas about money: how one makes money, how one manages money, how someone with a lot of money behaves, and how much is enough money, for example. These scripts arise from our experiences with money in our families and our communities. Whether we realize it or not, these primary messages influence us and may work against us in our quest for wealth.

Why Some People Spend for Love

Money scripts that you carry from your childhood can play an important role in your ability to save money. For example, if you were raised in a household where emotional connection between family members was poor, but things in the form of presents were used as a replacement for love, you may see the acquisition of things as a way to feel loved. This often happens subconsciously and can override more sensible decisions. You may feel compelled to buy things to feel loved, which will make it much harder for you to save money.

Consider the kinds of messages you may have received. Did your father tell you that wealthy people were rude and arrogant and didn't understand or value the important things in life? Did your mother express the idea that women are helpless when it comes to making and managing money? Did your family always live close to the financial edge, or was there always enough for your needs—and some of your wants?

You can examine these messages and their effects on you and challenge them so that you can make different decisions about wealth than you have in the past. For example, if your mother thought that women shouldn't be involved in financial decision-making and left it up to your father, that doesn't have to be your approach, even if it worked for your mother. If your family always lived close to the edge, then you may also feel comfortable living close to the edge. But consider that moving away from the edge could be fulfilling in its own way.

What Your Money Scripts Say

Fill in the blanks below to take a reading on whether your (conscious or unconscious) ideas about money are holding you back.

1. Wealthy people get that way because _____

   _____

2. People are poor because _____

   _____

3. Financially I am entitled to _____

   _____

4. The relationship between money and happiness is _____

   _____

5. I will always be able to afford to _____

   _____

6. I could never afford to _____

   _____

7. Financially I do not deserve _____

   _____

8. Parents owe their children _____

   _____

9. Never trust your money to _____

   _____

10. I am afraid to have considerable wealth because _____

   _____

Note that questions 6–10 reflect money limitation beliefs. As you work your way through this book, you will learn how these negative thought patterns—and everything negative, or perhaps just limiting, that you've already uncovered about your money script—can significantly interfere with your goal of wealth creation.

Do You Have What It Takes to Be Rich?

Numerous studies have reported that individuals, irrespective of gender, who create wealth exhibit many, if not all, of the following characteristics:

- Focused and goal directed
- Passionate
- Creative
- Confident
- Energized by challenges
- Hard working
- Disciplined
- Able to motivate and direct others
- Innovative
- Informed
- Charismatic
- Risk takers
- Ability to choose long-term satisfaction over immediate gratification

Okay, so you do have work to do! The whole goal of this book is to help you train your brain to foster these characteristics. So read on, aspirants.

IF YOU WANT TO GET RICH, GET HAPPY!

We live in a culture that strongly equates the abundance of money with happiness—even though we know all rich people aren't happy. Psychologists and researchers have consistently proven that being positively energized (happy) leads to better performance, increased creativity, self-confidence, energy, and brainpower. This achievable combination vastly improves your chances of acquiring wealth and achieving whatever levels of success you value. In fact, when your brain is feeling optimistic and energized, it will function far more effectively than when you are feeling negative or depressed—that's just a given.

Go for the Experience

Researchers Leaf van Boven of the University of Colorado and Cornell's Thomas Gilovich have found that we're happier when we choose experiences over material things. Whether it's vacationing in Italy, photographing local wildlife, playing the piano, or learning new subject matter, activities that fully engage our minds fulfill core self-determination needs. "Experiences contribute to the process of self-actualization," Van Boven reported. "They help people become the type of people they would like to become." Which means it's not the things you can buy in life, but the experiences you can create that enhance the brain activity that contributes to ultimate success. Brains were designed for novelty and challenge and thrive on stimulation and engagement.

Cash In on Happiness

Studies have shown that once you're able to meet your needs (live comfortably above poverty level) having money doesn't correlate to happiness. But studies have also shown that people who are happy tend to earn more money. How does that happen?

Feeling happy keeps your brain chemistry more even, rather than plummeting up and down as stress hormones rise or fall. Other than being much more relaxed, here are additional reasons why being happy matters, particularly in relation to your brain's health. Being happy:

- stimulates the growth of nerve connections
- increases mental productivity
- improves your ability to analyze and think
- affects your view of your surroundings
- increases attentiveness

In short, happy thoughts lead to more happy thoughts, and happy people are more creative, solve problems faster, and tend to be more mentally alert.

Being happy is just one of the skills you can master that will empower and embolden you—and your brain—on your quest for wealth.

IS WEALTH YOUR DESTINY?

Humans are the only species known to have a conscious awareness that we have brains and bodies capable of adaptability, that we can affect the course our lives take, that we can make choices along the way that vastly affect the quality of our lives—biologically, intellectually, environmentally, and spiritually. As humans, we have the ability to mold our very beings to become what or who we wish to become. While some of us may, indeed, have genetic and biological imperatives that may require medication or training to overcome, or at least to modulate, the vast majority of us do, in fact, hold our destiny in our hands.

Name Three Things That Can Create More Wealth

One study found that people who were asked to write down three very specific things that made them happy each day, for a week, were happier than those who didn't. This trend continued throughout one-, three-, and six-month check-ins, and long after the study ended. Researchers believe the people who focused on three specific things that brought them happiness each day essentially trained their brains to look for things that made them happy. You can use this same concept by looking for three things you did each day to increase your wealth and thereby train your brain to look for opportunities to create more wealth.

Yes, you can absolutely train your brain to succeed, to accomplish what you want in life, to become the best you, to make measured financial decisions, to maximize its function in relation to achieving your dreams, and so on. It will require focus, intention, dedication, accountability, action, and persistence, but you can reshape your brain to experience and create greater wealth.

We'll provide very specific actions you can take to tune up your brain, to better balance emotions and rational thinking when making decisions, to stimulate your brain to grow and expand, to nourish your brain, and so on. As for now, here's the bad news and the good news when it comes to brain transformation in relation to getting rich:

The Bad News:

- Your brain has evolved slowly and still reverts to ancient responses, which can unnerve and thwart your best efforts upon occasion.
- Your brain is hard-wired to feel and react quickly and instinctively to fear; reflection comes in third, long after panic has set in.
- Unless challenged, your brain will settle into neuronal ruts.
- Your brain will degenerate: Unused synapses will dissipate and no new synapses will form unless challenged.
- Your brain chemistry can create unbalanced behavior.
- Drugs and alcohol can severely affect your brain function.
- Your brain loses certain firepower as you age (but gains new abilities).

The Good News:

- Your brain is at your service.
- Damaged brains are capable of regeneration.
- Your brain will create new synapses when new activities require them.
- Your brain will bolster and reinforce existing neuronal pathways, as needed.
- Your brain can be rewired, employing atypical regions to perform required tasks.
- You can do things that will improve your brain chemistry; and, if necessary, you can use medication to improve brain function and emotional reactivity.
- Your mind can teach your brain to tamp down fear.
- You can train your brain to focus, learn new skills, and grow.

- You can do things that will help your brain remain supple and healthy.
- Older brains do become wiser brains. It's never too late to learn new tricks.

Sounds pretty good at the end, doesn't it? That's because there's a wealth of actions you can take to train your brain to get rich, and we're going to talk about a great many ideas and ways to execute them, but first you need to know the basics about your brain and how it works. Turn the page, and you'll be taking the first step on your journey to a wealthier life!

CHAPTER 2

HOW YOUR BRAIN WORKS

Principle: Your magnificent brain is at your service.

Your brain is, by far, the most complex organ in your body, capable of making tens of thousands of calculations in a second and working faster than any manmade supercomputer. You can leverage these calculations to build your wealth.

Your highly complex brain:

- Monitors and controls your breathing, heartbeat, blood circulation, digestion, and all other body functions
- Feels, interprets, and responds to pressure, pain, arousal, etc.
- Coordinates all muscle movements
- Experiences and executes a wide range of moods
- Observes, interprets, creates, stores, and recalls myriad complex memories
- Connects memories and thoughts to form complex associations
- Performs abstract thinking
- Creates and integrates your identity
- Regenerates brain cells

And that's the short list! If it sounds like a broker on the floor of the stock exchange, you're right.

Like any other organ, or even like any more familiar machine, all of your brain parts, from small to large, contribute to keeping your brain in its best possible shape. Understanding how all of those parts ideally work together to create a healthy, fully functioning, regenerative, and growing brain gives you the knowledge to turn your brain into a finely oiled machine that functions at its maximum capacity to create a healthy, happy, and wealthy *you*. Some of the following details may be difficult to grasp when you first read them, but the better you understand them, the better you can direct your energies and personalize how you will train your brain to get rich!

ARE YOU UP TO SPEED?

So, you think you know a lot about your brain? Well, before we take you on a guided tour of the inner workings of your brain, take this quick true or false quiz to see if you're really up to speed.

The *What I Know About My Brain* Quiz

Mark items either true or false:

1. The human brain has evolved dramatically in the last 200,000 years.
2. The human brain is fully formed at birth and doesn't change much thereafter.
3. The human brain consists of 500 million neuron cells.
4. At least 50 percent of the human brain's neurons are found in the basal ganglia.

5. The most highly evolved part of the human brain is the limbic brain.
6. The CEO of the human brain is the cerebellum.

Answer Key

1. **F:** The human brain has not evolved dramatically in the last 200,000 years, which is why your instinctual, or reactive brain often overrules your prefrontal cortex, or thinking brain. Your neocortical brain has evolved, but we're all playing catch-up when dealing with modern life.
2. **F:** Although scientists believed this for many years, in recent years they have discovered that your brain is capable of change—throughout your life.
3. **F:** Your brain consists of over 100 billion cells (10 billion are neurons; 90 billion are "helper" cells).
4. **F:** Fully 50 percent of your brain's neurons are packed in your cerebellum, often referred to as your "little brain."
5. **F:** The most highly evolved part of your brain is your frontal lobe. It's the part of your brain that makes you most human because it allows you to think about yourself, something that animals cannot do.
6. **F:** The CEO of your brain is your frontal lobe, particularly your prefrontal cortex (PFC), where all of your brain-mind functions are integrated.

YOUR BRAIN PORTFOLIO

The most crucial part of a working brain is also its most basic: the brain cells known as neurons, their billions of helper cells, and how these cells interact with each other. Your brain consists of more than 100 billion cells (10 billion are neurons; 90 billion are "helper" cells) whose primary function is to form synapses for the exchange of electrical information.

100 Trillion and Counting

To get a visual idea of the size of your brain, put your two palms together and then make your hands into fists. When you look down at your thumbs, you can see the approximate size of your brain. Your curled up fingers even look a bit like the wrinkles in the surface of your brain. Its 100 billion nerve cells weigh about three pounds in total and connect with each other along 100 trillion different pathways.

Luckily, your neurons are not bundled into an unorganized mess, communicating information at random. Much like a finely tuned, functional corporation, your brain is organized into different "departments" that specialize in certain types of information—from basic survival information about your body's overall health and present condition to more complex areas that are concerned with thoughts, emotions, and reactions.

Money Junction

Each neuron has a central body, or nucleus, where cellular metabolism takes place, but it also has incredibly long, stretched-out "arms" (known as axons) and smaller "arms" (known as dendrites). Under a microscope, these "arms" seem to be oscillating in waves. When an electrical impulse builds up enough steam, it travels the short distance from the dendrites to the tip of the axon, where a chemical messenger, known as a neurotransmitter, is released to assist the electrical impulse in binding to receptor sites on dendrites on other neurons.

This junction is called a synapse, and each cell is capable of generating approximately 15,000 synapses, which altogether equates to a vast network of axons creating around 100 trillion synapses.

Your Brain's Three Sections

In general, there are three major areas of the brain, each containing many structures that work together toward a common goal:

1. **Reptilian.** Your reptilian brain is the most ancient part of your brain, meaning it likely formed the entire brain of early man. It operates behind the scenes and contains all the brain structures that regulate your survival needs: food, oxygen, heart rate, blood pressure, and reproduction, among many others. It's like a silent sentinel that monitors your body and surroundings without your conscious knowledge. Your fight-or-flight response, reflexive actions, and other instinctual behaviors all generate from this part of your brain.

2. **Limbic.** Your limbic brain sits on top of your reptilian brain and most likely developed as man evolved. It helps you focus on your emotional life and the formation of memories. Your limbic system contains structures responsible for sensations of pleasure and pain, happiness and fear, and is very responsive to hormones and drugs, such as opiates like morphine. Limbic structures become highly activated when you dream. Your limbic system provides the gateway to the formation of powerful, emotional memories and compels you to seek sensations that make you happy or fill you with pleasure.

3. **Neocortex.** This is your "higher" brain, which is also sometimes called your cortex. It's the part of the brain you have seen a million pictures of because it sits on top of and surrounds your limbic brain; it resembles a gelatinous wrinkled mushroom cap. The neocortex is responsible for planning, abstract thoughts, and reasoning. It's the part of your brain that senses and perceives the world around you, allows you to formulate reactions, and allows you to think about thinking. Your personality, your hopes, and even your ability to speak all generate from—and reside within—your neocortex.

Wrinkles Pay Off

When you look at pictures of the brain, one of the things you'll notice first is that the surface of your neocortex is covered with what appear to be wrinkles. These wrinkles aren't signs of age; they're an evolutionary adaptation. Having wrinkles and folds in the surface of your brain allows for the surface area to be many times larger than it would be if your brain was smooth; the wrinkles allow us to pack many millions more neurons within our skulls. They let us make more neuron associations and give us a great ability to learn and make new connections as we age.

THE FIVE MAJOR AREAS OF YOUR NEOCORTEX (OR CORTEX) AND THEIR FUNCTIONS

Because your cortex surrounds and covers your reptilian and limbic brains, a surgeon would have to remove this part of the brain, or cut into it, in order to see many of the other structures underneath. It's so large and contains so many of your highest-order functions that neuroscientists have divided the neocortex into four lobes (based on the type of information each manages) and the cerebellum, or "little brain."

1. Your frontal lobe
2. Your temporal lobe
3. Your parietal lobe
4. Your occipital lobe
5. Your cerebellum

These lobes are divided into left and right halves, or hemispheres, by the central sulcus, which runs lengthwise down the center of your brain. For the most part, the left and right halves of these lobes are responsible for similar functions, but each focuses on opposite sides of your body. The left side of your brain is concerned with the right side of your body, and the right side of your brain is responsible for the left side of your body.

In addition to these four cerebral lobes, many neuroscientists also include the cerebellum—literally your "little brain"—as a fifth major area.

Yes, it's complicated, but hang in with us as we describe what each area of your brain does. Getting to know the parts of your brain will vastly improve your ability to understand how it functions overall and what you can do to protect and improve your brain functions and thereby utilize it to create wealth.

Your Frontal Lobe

At the very front of your brain lies an area known as the frontal lobe. It is the largest of the lobes—about 30 percent of your brain's overall size—and is the most highly evolved portion of your brain. It is the frontal lobe that makes us human. It controls most of your executive decision-making, serves as the seat of your personality, and is the part of your brain that allows you to think about yourself. Some call the frontal cortex "the CEO of your brain" because it is responsible for double-checking decisions and actions and giving the final okay before you interact with the rest of the world.

Change Your Connections, Change Your Prosperity

Albert Einstein's brain was preserved for many years after his death. Upon examination, neuroscientists discovered that the world's most famous genius experienced different changes in his brain than most other brains. Notably, the area that separated his temporal lobe from his parietal lobe was almost completely gone, and neuroscientists believe that this could account for his more integrative way of thinking and his ability to make unusual associations that other, "more normal" people couldn't see. A researcher from the University of California–Berkeley also found that Einstein had more brain connections in these "logical" brain parts than other men. Einstein's brain shows us that changing your connections, and the structure of your brain, really *can* help you think differently, more logically, and with more clarity!

Your Prefrontal Cortex

At the heart of the frontal lobe is an area known as the prefrontal cortex (or PFC), which is likewise divided into left and right halves, or hemispheres. This area sits directly behind the center of your forehead and is the last to develop as you grow into an adult. Although teenagers like to think they have fully formed brains, the prefrontal cortex is still growing and doesn't really begin to shine until postadolescence. On average, this process begins and finishes about a year earlier in girls as compared to boys.

This prefrontal cortex serves as the integration center of all of your brain-mind functions. In other words, it not only regulates the signals that your neurons transmit to other brain parts and to your body, but it allows you to think about and reflect upon what you are physically doing. In particular, the PFC allows you to control your emotional responses through connections to your deep limbic brain. It gives you the ability to focus on whatever you choose and to gain insight about your thinking processes. The PFC is the only part of your brain that can control your emotions and behaviors and help you focus on whatever goals you elect to pursue. It helps you grow as a human being, change what you wish to change, and live life the way *you* decide!

Your Orbitofrontal Cortex

Your orbitofrontal cortex (OFC) is a subdivision of your PFC, and is defined anatomically as the part of the PFC that sits directly above the orbits of the eye (hence "orbital" frontal). It has been historically one of the least-understood regions of the human brain, but recent research has suggested that it is important for decision-making, expectation (of both good and bad consequences) and particularly in assigning the relative value of objects, people, and experiences to the individual. It is your OFC that understands the *value* of money and is going to be important for letting you make decisions based on both subjective and objective worth. Quite a task for such a narrow part of the brain!

The Temporal Lobe

As the name suggests, the temporal lobe is the part of your brain that resides under your temples on either side of your head, just behind and below the frontal cortex (thus, there are actually two separate temporal cortices). Your temporal lobes provide some sensory processing, most notably hearing, and contain the areas of your brain that are responsible for both speaking and understanding speech.

However, each of the temporal lobes also houses its attendant hippocampus. Each of your two hippocampi converts short-term memories into long-term memories for storage and is critical for the formation of new factual or emotional experiences. Alzheimer's plaques, for example, begin in the cortex near the hippocampus and then enter the hippocampus. Memory loss is often the first sign of Alzheimer's disease.

Your temporal lobe serves as the gateway to thoughts and experiences and determines how they are processed and stored in your mind. Many mood disorders emerge from the dysfunction of the temporal lobe and the inability to process memories correctly. A fully functioning temporal lobe makes for a sharper you!

The Parietal Lobe

The two halves of your parietal lobe rest at the top of your brain, just behind your frontal lobe and above your temporal lobes. This parietal lobe handles the bulk of sensory integration, receiving information from different types of sensation—like touch—and creating a smooth data stream that works together in real time. Your parietal lobes also provide your sense of where you are in the world (known to neuroscientists as *proprioception*). It basically helps you navigate your way through your day-to-day life without bumping into walls.

Your parietal lobe is also where knowledge and reasoning concerning numbers takes place, and thus it is very important in the goal of making all those dollars add up! Many neuroscientists agree that, since many types of fact-based senses are integrated in the parietal lobes (i.e., *where* you are in the world, *what* you are looking at, *how* you are going to make an action to respond), this lobe is concerned with the logical aspects of interacting with the world, and it will be important to you in your quest to be more successful.

The Occipital Lobe

The two halves of the occipital lobe sit at the rear of your brain, just behind and below the parietal lobes, at the back of your head. This part of the brain is concerned with processing all of the visual information coming into your brain from your eyes. Since we humans tend to rely on our vision more than any other sense, we have an entire lobe of the brain dedicated to processing detailed visual information.

The Cerebellum

Your cerebellum, often referred to as your "little brain," sits underneath the occipital lobes and parietal lobes and is a distinctly different cluster of cells that are separate from your four lobes. Fully 50 percent of all of the brain's neurons are packed into this little region, which is important in motor control, your ability to pay attention, and experiencing basic emotional responses, such as fear and pleasure.

Much of the cerebellum's input is centered upon fine-tuning your actions to the outside world, making sure that you walk in a straight line or grasp your fingers with the right amount of pressure around a delicate eggshell, for example. It computes a lot of information in a very small space, and recently neuroscientists have come to realize that the cerebellum is also pivotal in other learning processes, most of which are largely subconscious. A professional baseball player moving his hand to catch a line drive uses his cerebellum much in the same way that you respond to a sudden, loud sound by reflexively jumping. Both of these responses arise from action patterns that rely on the cerebellum, as do many of your basic emotional responses.

DEEPER BRAIN STRUCTURES

The neocortex is large and imposing, and the many functions it handles are the ones that are most instantly recognizable:

- It is important for how we think about ourselves and connect to the outside world.
- It contains all the functions we recognize as distinctly human: language, the ability to think and reason, verbal communication, complicated learning, and abstract thinking.

However, the neocortex only makes up one-third of your brain, and the many parts that lie underneath it hold the key to some of our most important functions. These structures are usually known as "deep" brain areas, since you need to "dive" under the neocortex in order to find them. Most of the areas of your limbic system, or emotional brain, are located in these deep places.

Anterior Cingulate Cortex

The name of this brain region is a mouthful (as was its former name, anterior cingulate gyrus), but it describes exactly where it is and what it looks like. "Anterior" indicates that it is close to the front of the brain, located just behind your frontal lobes. "Cingulate" is Latin for "belt" and thus describes how this region "wraps around" another deep brain structure called the corpus callosum. "Gyrus" originated from the Latin word *gyre*, meaning a circle or turning. Taken together, this accurately describes this brain region as a forward area that surrounds other, lower brain structures and is turned or bent like a fold.

The anterior cingulate cortex is situated right between the decision-making frontal cortex and the emotional limbic brain, where it performs as an emotional gear-shifter. It brings information concerning emotions, empathy, and reward from the lower limbic brain structures to the prefrontal cortex. Once the information is processed in the prefrontal cortex, a reaction to the information and a plan for action is delivered back down through the anterior cingulate cortex to the limbic brain.

Thus, emotional and rational information is ramped up or ramped down depending on the amount of information passing through this cortex. By learning to strengthen your prefrontal cortex's ability to control emotional responses, you can train your brain to increase the neuronal connections sent back down to suppress unwanted or negative emotional states arising from the deeper limbic structures. Achieving this will allow your brain to shift more easily into goal-oriented, rather than fear or emotionally oriented behavior. Think of it as the broker between your emotional self and your rational self—your anterior cingulate cortex can be a game-changer in terms of making yourself more successful and focused.

The Deep Limbic System

Sharing a connection to the anterior cingulate cortex, this walnut-sized area contains the thalamus, hypothalamus, and the amygdala. Each performs important functions:

- **Thalamus:** Located at the top of the brain stem, it relays messages from the spinal cord up to the cerebrum and back down the spinal cord to your nervous system.
- **Hypothalamus:** Also located at the base of the brain, it maintains many of your body's hormones and monitors bodily functions, like blood pressure, body temperature, body weight, and appetite.
- **Amygdala:** Lies deep in the center of your limbic brain and is the size of an almond. It is in charge of many basic and

emotionally charged needs, including love and sex. It triggers strong emotions, like anger, fear, love, lust, jealousy, and so on. More recently, it has been connected to depression and even autism. It's often slightly larger in males, enlarged in sociopathic brains, and diminishes slightly in size as you age.

Your deep limbic system is an older part of your mammalian brain, which was the first to enable animals and humans to experience and express emotions. It is responsible for passion, emotion, and desire, all of which add emotional spice to our lives in both positive and negative ways.

In general, when your deep limbic system is quieted, or less active, you experience a positive, more hopeful state of mind. When your deep limbic system is heated up, or overactive, negativity can take over. This emotional coloring of events is critical, as the importance you give to events in your life drives you to action (such as avidly pursuing something that makes you happy or motivated) or causes avoidance behavior (withdrawing from something that has frightened or hurt you in the past).

Basal Ganglia

Your basal ganglia are a series of brain areas, or "nuclei," that are classified into two sets that serve distinct functions:

The first set (consisting of the striatum, pallidum, substantia nigra, and subthalamic nucleus) is concerned with motor control. Currently, these basal ganglia regions are thought to be primarily involved with "action selection," making a quick decision between several possible reaction plans, for instance, deciding to take a quick step left if someone is riding a bike towards you on the pavement, rather than stepping backwards or doing a somersault.

The second set, collectively known as the limbic nuclei of the basal ganglia, consists of the nucleus accumbens, the ventral pallidum, and the ventral tegmental area. These three areas play an important role in determining sensations of reward and anxiety, particularly via the connections between the ventral tegmental area and the nucleus accumbens. Many addictive drugs, such as cocaine, amphetamines, and nicotine, affect this pathway, as do more natural rewards like savoring excellent food and enjoying sex.

What Are MRI and fMRI?

MRI (Magnetic Resonance Imaging) is a radiology technique that uses a powerful magnetic field to scan soft tissues of the body, like the brain. An fMRI (functional MRI) measures the change in blood flow related to brain activity in real time. This helps scientists discover which areas of the brain respond to what activities and in tracking changes in the brain.

Further, the brains of people anticipating a win at the roulette table appear to react much like those taking euphoria-inducing drugs. Gamblers and people prone to high-risk money strategies show blood flow changes in these limbic brain regions similar to that seen in cocaine addicts in fMRI experiments. The changes even varied in accordance with the amount of money involved! Thus, your deep limbic nuclei are a powerful force to be reckoned with, as they can have a lot of sway over your emotional response to gaining and losing money.

CHEMICAL MESSENGERS

Your brain consists of a network of neurons whose sole responsibility is to transmit signals from cell to cell. These signals are electrically transported within a single neuron and chemically transported between neurons. Neurotransmitters deliver the chemical messages. There are many different kinds of neurotransmitters, and thus they are able to transmit gradients of information more easily than a simple electrical signal. Some neurotransmitters deliver fairly straightforward, simple messages.

Other neurotransmitters are more complex and have different functions in different brain areas, and these types of neurotransmitters are often called *neuromodulators*. Three of the more well-known neuromodulators are dopamine, serotonin, and acetylcholine. Dopamine and serotonin, in particular, are known to be key neurotransmitters in the regulation of pleasure, happiness, rewarding situations, and mood. Acetylcholine in the brain has been shown to be important in shifting from sleep to wakefulness and helps in sustaining attention and forming memories, especially in the hippocampus.

Even small changes in the number of neuromodulators that transmit signals from neuron to neuron can have a noticeable impact on your mood, disposition, and thought processes. For example, many addictive drugs and behaviors (such as gambling) overstimulate the dopamine system and lead to abnormal behaviors, both during the high, when the addictive drug or behavior causes dopamine levels to soar, and during the low, when the addictive drug or behavioral experience has been cleared from your system and dopamine levels subside.

Having too much or too little dopamine has also been implicated in behavior disorders from attention deficit hyperactivity disorder (ADHD) to schizophrenia. Changes in the balance of serotonin in your brain can also lead to mood disorders, such as clinical depression, anxiety attacks, and phobias. Thus, having the right balance of neurotransmitters allows for your brain to hum along, operating at its full capacity with *you* in control.

Now that your brain is fired up, let's move on to the next chapter, where you'll learn about recent breakthroughs in neuroscience that will help you generate greater wealth!

CHAPTER 3

BREAKTHROUGHS IN NEUROSCIENCE THAT WILL SUPPORT YOUR QUEST FOR WEALTH

Principle: It's a whole new world in neuroscience, and that knowledge can hold the key to maximizing your brainpower and attaining wealth.

In the last decade, neuroscientists have made startling discoveries about the human brain and its capabilities. Throughout this chapter, we'll discuss the ones that are most relevant to your quest for wealth, such as the ability to create new circuitry, tamp down overly reactive emotions, and use imagination to create your desired reality. In fact, your brain is more pliable and adaptable than you might have imagined—and your mind absolutely has the ability to guide and direct your brain, making it a productive, hardworking partner in your quest for wealth, as you'll learn throughout the book.

Until recently, for example, scientists believed that the human brain and its structures were formed during gestation and infancy and remained pretty much unchanged through childhood: You had a given number of neurons in a specific brain structure, and while the number might vary among people, once you were done with childhood development, your connections were already made, and the learning and growing period of your brain was over. In the last decade, however, researchers have found significant evidence that this previously held assumption is not actually so, and that something called *neuroplasticity* continues throughout our lives.

MOLD YOUR BRAIN

Neuroscientists use the word "plastic" to mean a material has the ability to change, to be molded into different shapes. Thus, neuroplasticity is your brain's ability to alter its physical structure, to repair damaged regions, to grow new neurons and get rid of old ones, to rezone regions that performed one task and have them assume a new task, and to change the circuitry that weaves neurons into the networks that allow us to remember, feel, suffer, think, imagine, and dream.

Scientists now believe that throughout your life, your brain can continue to:

1. **Reactivate unused circuitry.** The expression "it's like riding a bike" is very true when it comes to your brain. Most of the time, you'll never completely forget a skill once learned, though you might need a short period of practice to kick your neurons back into gear.
2. **Create new circuitry.** For instance, some of the neurons in your nose responsible for smell are made new and replaced every few weeks, and new neurons are made in other parts of your brain as well. Also, whenever you learn something new, your brain can strengthen existing neuronal connections and create new synapses that allow you to maximize new skills.

3. **Rewire circuitry.** Parts of your brain that were used for one purpose can be retasked to other uses. This is often the case with stroke victims who relearn to use a limb or to speak after some neurons are destroyed.

4. **Quiet aberrant circuits and connections.** (such as those leading to depression, posttraumatic stress disorder (PTSD), obsessive-compulsive disorder (OCD), phobias, and so on). Some parts of your brain can exert control over others and change how much they affect your mood, decision-making, and thought processes.

How Does Neuroplasticity Contribute to Getting Rich?

Because of your brain's plasticity, you can train it to do whatever it needs to do, regardless of your age. Here's why:

1. The actions you take can literally expand or contract different regions of the brain, firing up circuits or tamping them down. Example: If you worry excessively, you are activating certain types of pathways due to habit. You can learn, however, to retrain your brain to quiet these pathways and strengthen others, so it doesn't automatically go down the "worry" highway the moment you sense a problem. You can't make good financial decisions if you're worrying too much.

2. The more you ask your brain to do, the more space it sets up to handle the new tasks, often by shrinking or repurposing space that houses your ability to perform rarely used tasks. Example: If you typically go into a melancholy funk or choose an "old reliable" solution when you face financial problems, your brain will continue that habit. If, however, you instruct your brain to come up with creative solutions, whether it's boosting your income or making smart investment decisions,

you can shut down the old pathways by making them less used and smaller, and instead open up and increase use of the creativity workshop in your brain.

3. New brain-scanning technology has shown that conscious perception activates the same brain areas as imagination. In effect, you can ease the long-term effects of painful memories by rewriting (or more correctly, rewiring) the past that lives within your brain. So if you're haunted by bad financial decisions or past failures, you can rewire those memories and focus on imagining a brighter future.

4. Your brain usually cannot reliably distinguish between recorded experience and internal fantasy. If you program your mind with images of you being successful and spend time visualizing the desired images long enough and hard enough, your brain will think those images really happened and that you are already successful.

In other words, whatever you ask your brain to do (employing intention, focus, practice, and reinforcement), it will strive to do. It is a tool you can use in whatever way you see fit. The more often you ask your brain to think the types of thoughts that will create wealth, the more your brain responds by forging new or beefing up existing neuronal circuitry to light up your wealth and success boards, and by weakening the neuronal connections that drain your wealthy thoughts.

You can train your brain to bury the unproductive, depressing thoughts and habits that drag you (and your brain) down and to shine light on, nourish, and reinforce the productive thoughts and activities that recharge your motivational and creative batteries. Here's the beauty in it: By using your thoughts and choosing certain activities, you can lay the groundwork for brain restructuring that will make you wealthier.

THINKING PROSPEROUS THOUGHTS

Even more exciting, recent breakthroughs in neuroscience have also shown that your brain can reshape itself and form new synapses purely from thinking thoughts. What you think about and how you think matter; your thoughts can create new realities. Scientific evidence shows that if you envision it—thoroughly and often enough—it can come.

You can think thoughts that reshape your brain, and although outside activities or influences often assist by imprinting and boosting the process, none are *required*. If you think the necessary thoughts—thereby training your brain to act in a new way, strongly *willing* it to do so—and then reinforce this new way of thinking, your brain can change itself, *and* the way it works, to fall in alignment with your thoughts.

What does all this mean? It means that what you think, do, and say matters—and that it affects who you become on the outside, on the inside, *and* in your brain. Mostly, it means that you can retrain your brain to be more productive, more resilient, more thoughtful, and more creative.

GROUNDBREAKING STUDIES

New studies in the field of neuroscience are continually revealing the intricacies of how our brains work, and we want to mention a few groundbreaking study results that are shedding light on how you can train your brain to get rich.

The Role Valuation and Imagination Play in Making Decisions

Evaluation is a fundamental process of human thought, necessary for making decisions whether they relate to choosing products, making appropriate responses to situations, and even determining one's life goals. Research has indicated that the brain's orbitofrontal cortex (OFC), which is part of the PFC, plays a central role in evaluating choices. This part of your brain seems to understand "value" in all its forms, whether you are working for something directly important to your survival (like food, water, or shelter) or something that's a little more abstract and can *represent* a reward (like money or tokens). Importantly—and this is really key—recent research has confirmed that you can activate this part of your brain, or any part of your brain, simply by *imagining it*. For example, in an interesting study conducted in 2002, Dr. Nakia Gordon at Bowling Green State University, Ohio, reported that people can relive past experiences and experience emotions simply by envisioning them, and the motions they performed while doing them. In the same vein, a group led by Dr. Will Cunningham from Ohio State University found that the OFC is activated when individuals were thinking about things that they value, and activating these brain areas leads to investing more neural circuitry, better understanding value, and *assigning* a value to anything you desire!

Results

In Dr. Cunningham's study, young men were asked to envision things that they either liked or disliked—objects, people, or situations. They concentrated on the subjective value of each of the things they were thinking about, that is, *how much* they liked or disliked it, and how much they wanted it. In doing so, different parts of the orbitofrontal cortex (OFC) lit up in response to thinking about valued things (something you could put a price on) and valued people. This showed the researchers that even though value might not always be equated with a hard number, the OFC was capable of taking *any* valued idea versus *any other* valued idea and comparing them.

Brain activity also showed involvement of brain areas typically associated with the generation of emotions along with the OFC, even though participants were told to make decisions only based on "value." Of course, "value" is subjective, and can involve sentimentality or good memories. All of these things were taken into consideration in this imagination exercise.

In the Bowling Green study of imagination and emotion, women who merely imagined the body movements associated with laughing and crying lit up the same brain areas that were activated if they were *actually* laughing and crying, and experiencing happy or sad emotions. That means that merely *imagining* moments of happiness or sadness was exactly the same to the brain as *actually* experiencing them.

How This Research Can Help You Get Rich

The findings of the Bowling Green and Ohio State University studies reveal that simply *imagining* valued items or experiences, without having any external cue, triggers the brain in *the exact same way* as actually having the object or experience—and can trigger the brain to think about value and reward. According to Dr. Cunningham, these results "support the idea that imagined stimuli . . . are evaluated in the OFC using a common system that has been identified in previous research for externally perceived stimuli." That means that merely imagining or focusing on a desired event or valued outcome, can make you *actually* exercise the brain "muscles" that make decisions about money—in a neurochemical sense!—and strengthen the evaluative connections in your brain.

You're Never Too Old to Get Rich!

Neurogenesis, literally meaning "birth of neurons," is the process by which neurons are formed and the entire brain is populated with neurons. While this phenomenon is most active before you are born, recent neuroscience has shown that this process continues through puberty, adolescence, and right into adulthood—virtually until you stop learning new skills. The idea of adult neurogenesis was slow to take hold in the neuroscience community—overthrowing a long-held belief (that it was all over in young adulthood) can sometimes be difficult!

The Neurogenesis Breakthrough

Here are various study results pertinent to neurogenesis:

1. The first evidence of adult neurogenesis in mammals was presented by Dr. Joseph Altman in 1962, where he provided solid evidence showing that new neurons formed in the brains of adult rats following brain damage.
2. Dr. Altman followed this initial study with similar demonstrations of adult neurogenesis in a brain area called the hippocampus in 1963.
3. In 1969, Dr. Altman further discovered and named the source of adult-generated neurons in the olfactory bulb, a portion of the brain dedicated to the perception of odors. However, Dr. Altman's careful studies were overwhelmingly ignored by the scientific community at large!
4. In the late 1980s and the 1990s, Altman's work came back into the spotlight and was replicated and expanded upon by other researchers, such as Dr. Shirley Bayer, Dr. Michael Kaplan, and Dr. Fernando Nottebohm. In studying the brains of mammals and birds, these researchers showed that adult neurogenesis takes place in several brain areas in these animal species, and in the 1990s, human neurogenesis was confirmed.

New Neurons Equal New Money

These landmark studies proved a simple and profound truth: *Your brain can make new neurons.* While most of the early studies showed that new neurons were made in response to brain damage (similar to a stroke), further studies have shown that new neurons are made in many animals in response to experience and training regimens. Furthermore, your neurons can *change.* They are plastic and flexible, and can strengthen their connections in a matter of minutes. Yes, in the time it takes you to read this paragraph, your brain can be set on the road to change, to becoming smarter and richer!

Fire Together, Wire Together, Wealthy Ever After

Canadian psychologist Dr. Donald Hebb coined a phrase known to neuroscientists the world over: "Neurons that fire together, wire together." This concept describes, in a nutshell, how we learn and how we come to associate things with each other. In other words, it describes how *mental activity changes neural structure,* or how what you think changes your brain! Dr. Hebb developed the theory that it is the timing of neuronal firing that makes for new or changed wiring. Neurons that fire within a few thousandths of a second of each other—basically, neurons that are firing at the same time in response to a thought or experience— can do one of two things: They can strengthen existing synapses or build new synapses.

Hebb's Law

Dr. Hebb combined data from anatomical, behavioral, and psychological analyses of the early twentieth century into a single statement: When neuron A is close to neuron B, and neuron A repeatedly is stimulated enough in order to excite neuron B, some metabolic change occurs that makes neuron A more likely than other neurons to stimulate neuron B. In other words, those two neurons become more linked than the other neurons around them, and that connection takes up more available neural space than it did before.

Focus on Money

Dr. Hebb's research has provided fundamental knowledge to neuroscience, and even though Hebb's law was put to paper in 1949, the theory has held up after more than sixty years of research and countless experiments. What this means is that constant associations between neurons make those associations stronger. For example, if you routinely dwell on your past financial failures, unsuccessful ventures, lack of self-confidence, feelings of insecurity, and other negative patterns, the neurons involved in that particular mental activity will fire busily at the same time and automatically start wiring together as well. This process will add one more bit of neural structure to feeling uninspired, lazy, or inadequate.

On the other hand, if you regularly focus on the positive aspects of your personality and abilities, then the neurons involved in *those* thoughts will wire together and take up more space, stitching more hopefulness, confidence, and motivational energy into the fabric of your brain and yourself (and taking away space from the negative paths!).

It also means that the more time you spend thinking about money or ways to build wealth the more neuronal connections you'll make, wiring your brain for success.

Money Mindfulness

Richard Davidson, PhD, a prominent University of Wisconsin psychologist, has conducted several studies on the effects of a technique known as mindfulness meditation. Mindfulness meditation is the Buddhist practice of learning to focus your mind on being fully present in the here and now. (We'll discuss this further in Chapter 9.) In one of these studies, Davidson monitored the brain activity of three distinct groups of people: Tibetan Buddhist monks (who had logged 1,500 to 15,000 hours practicing mindfulness meditation, focused on compassion); people who had never meditated; and people who participated in an eight-week meditation training. Davidson and his researchers asked the participants to meditate on compassion and empathy while he monitored their brains.

PFC Carrot

The results of Davidson's study were startling. Among them:

1. When the people who had never meditated were asked to practice a Buddhist compassion meditation, on their first try, meditating stimulated their limbic system (emotional network).

2. When those who had never practiced meditation signed on for eight weeks, as the training progressed, their brains revealed more activity in the left prefrontal cortex (PFC), an area of the brain believed to be responsible not only for generating positive emotions, such as compassion, empathy, and happiness, but also extremely important for making decisions based on value and assigning emotional happiness to getting rewards (such as money!).

3. When Davidson studied the bran scans of the monks as they meditated, their scans showed significantly higher activity in their left PFCs, so much so the researchers were astounded, describing it as "well out of the normal range."

4. The monks also showed sustained changes in their baseline (i.e., without meditation) brain function, indicating that

their meditation practice had changed the way their brains functioned, even when not meditating. These changes were most evident in the left prefrontal cortex (PFC). Thus, by meditating, these monks were *permanently* changing the amount of activity in their PFC, increasing it, and making more connections that could be used towards evaluative judgments, which in your case would involve making better decisions about money and how to use it to get the most out of your life.

Think Rich, Get Rich

Davidson's studies demonstrate that, even with a relatively small amount of training, fully adult individuals were able to learn a technique that trained them to think differently and to beef up their neural connections in the place that mattered most: the CEO of the brain, the PFC. By training themselves to think differently than they had before, they actually rewired their brains, after only eight weeks.

The monks, who had had much more meditation practice, showed even more brain differences. The abnormally high activity in the left PFC of the monks suggests that they had formed new neuronal pathways and/or strengthened existing neural connections in this area simply by *thinking* about it. Meditation caused their brains to change, not only in response to active thought, but in a fundamental way all the time—even at baseline rest—without thinking about it. Meditation wired their brains for better decision-making and clarity of thought twenty-four hours a day—and it can help you too! Mindfulness meditation could help you make better decisions about money and how to use it to get the most out of your life by helping you rewire, grow, and strengthen your PFC and the neuronal pathways that play an essential role when making decisions about monetary value. Talk about the power of positive thinking!

All we can say is: Don't delay, your future awaits!

CHAPTER 4

NEURAL PATHWAYS TO WEALTH

Principle: You can use your mind to generate neural pathways in your brain and to strengthen neuronal connections that will facilitate your quest for wealth.

Every thought, perception, sensation, and emotion that expresses "you" has an electrical and chemical component: Genes, neuronal impulses, and neurotransmitters combine to express your personality as a sort of cocktail of emotional responses, drives, and memories. This "emotional cocktail" settles your brain into patterns, and often into habits. A habit forms a brain pathway simply because that particular neuronal pathway has been stimulated many times, usually because the original stimulation was perceived as positive. Habits effectively become a kind of addiction—an electrochemical itch that you feel compelled to scratch.

If you want to form new wealth-building habits or discard ones that haven't worked for you, you will have to consciously forge new, positively affiliated connections between the emotional limbic parts of your brain and your executive, or controlling, prefrontal cortex. Getting old neuron networks and new neuron networks—and the neurotransmitters associated with them—to work together to form smoother pathways often requires stimulating the brain with different activities, or different levels of activity, which we will discuss throughout this book. By changing nonproductive habits into productive habits—and reinforcing those habits—you can create new neural pathways in your brain that will make it easier for you to generate wealth.

ON THE MONEY WAVELENGTH

Different levels of activity are usually characterized as brain waves, which are pulses of activity that are occurring at regular intervals. Certain types of brain waves are associated with different electro-chemically active states and complexity of thinking. Some brain waves will help you generate wealth; others will dampen efforts.

Couch Potatoes Don't Get Rich

Psychophysiologist Thomas Mulholland found that after just *thirty seconds* of watching television, your brain begins to produce alpha waves, which indicate slow rates of activity. Alpha brain waves are associated with unfocused, receptive-only states of consciousness, which means that watching television represents one of the few instances in which you can achieve an alpha brain wave state with your eyes open. Basically, watching television is neurologically analogous to staring at a blank wall or sitting with your eyes closed, doing—and thinking—absolutely nothing.

Beta Brain, Active Brain

The mental activity normally associated with beta waves is the active awareness state that we experience from day to day at work and play. Beta brain waves kick in when you think logically, solve problems, and confront external stimuli. Beta brain waves have the ability to increase muscle tension, raise blood pressure, and create anxiety. It is not a state used in quiet reflection, but rather a state for getting things done. Dopamine is released more easily when your brain is in a beta frequency.

Alpha Brain, Sleepy Brain

These are the opposite of beta brain waves; alpha waves are prominent during relaxation, especially when your eyes are closed. Your brain moves in an alpha rhythm when you are day-dreaming or in a state of introspection. Alpha waves stimulate an increase in melatonin, which is a chemical often associated with sleepiness.

Theta Brain, Intuitive Brain

Theta brain waves engage your inner and intuitive subconscious. You'll find that your brain waves are in a theta frequency when you are going through memories or experiencing strong sensations and emotions, or reflecting upon emotional situations. Theta waves are also found when we are storing secrets, which we block out in times of pain, to survive what we feel unprepared to fix. Theta brain waves are often engaged when you sleep and are the equivalent of flexing emotional and dreaming brain muscles. People who have brain waves that often border between theta and beta frequencies are usually reported to be very extroverted and have low anxiety and low neuroticism: They seem to have found the balance between emotional and active, logical thinking. The neurotransmitter serotonin is often associated with theta brain waves, as is the neurotransmitter GABA (gamma-aminobutyric acid).

Delta Brain, Empathetic Brain

These are slower brain waves often associated with unconscious feelings and empathy. In healthy doses, these signals cause the right amount of empathy, but too much delta activity can force you to forget about yourself and your needs. Delta waves are the least well studied of the brain wave states, even though they are often associated with higher levels of serotonin.

Gamma Brain, Fast Brain

Gamma waves are without a doubt the fastest of the brain waves, operating at a frequency of 25–100 Hz (although usually found around 40 Hz). Neuroscientists only discovered them fairly recently, when those studying the visual system found that two unconnected neurons seemed to start to fire in time when an oscillation of about 40 Hz was reached. This is similar to a jazz musician playing a saxophone solo, while another musician is playing a different tune on the piano and they start playing the same notes, at the same time, in synchronized tandem. The more powerful the gamma wave, the more precise is the synchronization. Your brain areas—or your entire brain—in a gamma wave state tend to fire networks and form associations more quickly than a brain in any other state.

The formation of *gamma wave networks* could provide a vital clue as to how your brain may be able to change itself. When firing at an optimal speed, connections are formed more easily in an active mind. Allowing your brain to reach a gamma state could provide vital insights into how your brain can change itself, and how *you* can control the way in which it changes.

For example, during mindfulness meditation, monks far exceeded normal subjects when it came to the ability to generate intense, prolonged gamma wave activity in their prefrontal cortex, particularly on the left side. Because the prefrontal cortex sits in the executive chair of the mind, thus generating gamma wave activity in this area would allow for precise connections to be formed between the part of your brain that allows you to control your behavior and the more emotional, subconscious parts of your deeper limbic system.

Thus, stimulating your brain into the highest levels of activity through concentrated mindfulness, and focusing on yourself, your actions, and your reactions, could allow you to produce a state whereby the brain has the best chance to change into what *you* want it to be—wiser, more receptive to new ideas, more efficient, faster, healthier, and a wealth generator.

NEURONAL PATHWAYS TO SUCCESS

Thanks to brain plasticity—the near-miraculous ability to grow and change how your brain functions—you have it within your power to achieve a new focus and a new way of thinking. When you are able to see viable alternatives to what you perceive as limiting ways of thinking and acting, and are able to consciously adapt your thought patterns and behaviors, you will, over time, positively affect and change your brain's neural pathways and neurotransmitters, making your brain a more efficient machine capable of helping you more and more to achieve your goals— monetary and otherwise!

Engaging the specific areas of the brain that are responsible for emotional control and evaluative thinking—your left prefrontal cortex and orbitofrontal cortex, your anterior cingulate cortex, and your deep limbic structures—will provide a map for your pathways to success. By utilizing techniques such as focused concentration, mindfulness meditation, and behavioral adaptation (all of which we'll be discussing in later chapters), you can strengthen the neuronal connections focused on motivation, concentration, and creative thinking, and lower your responses to the emotional and often anxiety-ridden pathways that are likely undermining your ability to live an accomplished, wealthy, and fulfilling life.

SPECIFIC BRAIN AREAS RELATED TO WEALTH ACCUMULATION

Certain specific areas of your brain come into play when it comes to creating and sustaining financial wealth. Simply gaining an overview of the complex machinery that is your brain will lead to definite steps you can take to focus your brain on the acquisition and management of money, or whatever form of success you seek.

Your Prefrontal Cortex (PFC)

The prefrontal cortex is sometimes called the "executive" brain region, because it draws input from almost all the other regions, integrates them to form short- and long-term goals, and plans actions that take these goals into account. Your PFC is the brain region that has grown the most in the course of human evolution and which, therefore, most sharply differentiates you from your closest primate "relatives."

Even in the scientific arenas, your PFC is commonly called your brain's CEO. Because it's where input is integrated and actions are generated, it's also where emotional fights between greed and fear rage. It has several subdivisions (like any well-run corporation) that are meant for tackling different kinds of decision making. These subdivisions are:

1. Your ventral medial PFC, which burns brightly with the desire for making a killing or landing that really high-paying job, like becoming the hot-shot vice president in charge of sales, gung-ho and totally focused on scoring glory and hefty commissions.
2. Your orbitofrontal cortex (OFC), which is more evaluative and tries to assign an actual *value* to a gain. It's responsible for making the decisions about what is best for *you* out of

a number of different options, and tries to make balanced, rational decisions (like a good accountant!).

3. Your medial PFC, which can keep both of these areas in check by effectively tossing fear-soaked blankets on whatever has the other regions fired up. It is capable of dousing budding financial aspirations . . . if you let it!

Because it serves as your brain's CEO, the more you educate and stimulate all of the departments of your PFC, the more likely you are to make good investments, expand your career options, and learn new skills. The PFC can act as your emotional and intellectual moderator, helping you make sound financial decisions based on available facts, rather than making hasty decisions based on fear.

Your Amygdala

If your PFC is the calm, cool, and collected CEO of your brain, then your amygdala is like a stressed intern, fearful of every person that walks around the corner and prone to making impulsive, ill-informed decisions. This is where the fight-or-flight impulses duel. It's where taking a risk feels exciting and dangerous. Learning to quiet your amygdala leads to an increased ability to rely on your factual knowledge to weigh decisions, rather than falling sway to emotions. If your amygdala is all fired up, you may pass on good-but-mundane opportunities or blow other opportunities if you cannot tamp down rampant emotions. The good news: You can learn to quiet your amygdala.

Your Anterior Cingulate Cortex/Spindle Cells (ACC)

Your ACC houses neurons called "spindle cells." These cells are comparatively enormous, and very unique in the animal world (only humans, great apes, some species of whales, and elephants have been found to have them—and humans have the most of all, twice as many as great apes). The evolution of spindle cells has exploded in the last 200,000 years, most likely because they play such a large role in how the human brain functions and how our brains are distinguishable from those of other species.

Watch Your Ticker

We're all familiar with the stock market ticker, but did you know that there's also a neurological response called "ticking"? It's basically a phenomenon in which our own emotions tend to peak in synch with other people's reactions to the same experience or event. If you are feeling anxious about certain financial news, it's highly likely that many others are also feeling similarly. This can be a good thing or a bad thing. If the stock market is plummeting, before you punch the "sell" button, you might want to take ten or fifteen minutes to check your emotional ticker to see if you are responding to unsubstantiated fear running so high that other, less rational souls are panicking.

These cells are capable of latching on to signals from very wide-ranging parts of the brain and gathering them together—they can help information travel from the back to the front of your brain, from deep areas to cortex, etc. These cells are absolutely pivotal in helping your ACC focus attention, perceive pain, and detect errors from wide-ranging sources all at once.

Spindle cells also assist in the element of surprise when your normal expectations are shattered; it's more important to know about mistakes sooner than it is to know about successes. In an evolutionary sense, the hominids that reacted with the greatest surprise to the "least detectable differences" (smallest deviations from the norm) were the most likely to survive, which is why your ACC developed into an intuitive system built for speed, capable of responding in less than 3/10ths of a second . . . and why it remains far more sensitive to negative surprises than positive ones.

In studies in which subjects' brains were monitored as financial fortunes experienced ups and downs, 38 percent of the spindle cell neurons fired when the amount of money suddenly shrank, but only 13 percent were triggered when people got a larger than expected gain. And those spindle cell neurons that did fire to a positive surprise sent out weaker signals. Unfortunately, even though it seems like it should be the other way around, a positive surprise packs a lot less punch than a negative one.

Why Money Fires Up Your ACC

Even though it doesn't seem logical that your brain doesn't fully understand the concept of money, remember that money itself is a modern phenomenon, which means our brains haven't quite caught up. Your brain understands what money *represents*—what money has been associated with—but not money itself. Sensory input related to money and the emotions they generate still trigger a peculiarly primitive response when surprise is involved. When a surprise jolts your ACC, it can hit your hypothalamus, knocking your internal regulation out of kilter; and if these surprises happen on a large scale within a population, it can lead to stock market panic reactions. Studies have shown that the ACC fires much more intensely when errors resulted in monetary loss than it does when no money is at stake; and a wide swath of cells in the brain stem also switched on whenever a mistake cost money—showing that the spindle cells in the ACC have wide-ranging influence. When an identical error didn't have a monetary consequence, the brain stem barely responded.

The ACC is also sensitive to pattern repetition and reacts roughly three times more vigorously if a pattern reverses after eight repetitions than it does after a three-in-a-row pattern is broken. This search for patterns can be both positive and negative, so relying too heavily on your ACC is not the wisest course of action. Sometimes you need to consciously call upon your PFC to sort out the value of patterns and tamp down knee-jerk responses to historical patterning. Our rational mind knows that history does not always repeat itself, but our ACC "thinks" it does. We'll discuss this further in later chapters.

Nuclei (or Nucleus) Accumbens

There are two nucleus accumbens, which means nuclei is the proper plural name, but even neuroscientists tend to say "the nucleus accumbens" (even when they mean both). This is the seat of your reward center. It lights up when pleasurable emotions are anticipated and experienced. The more desirable the anticipated outcome, the more fiercely the neurons fire.

Our anticipation circuitry forces us to pay attention to the possibility of incoming rewards, but also leads us to expect that our future will *feel* better than it actually does when it finally occurs, which creates an emotional vacuum and explains why money does not really buy happiness.

Your nucleus accumbens compares learned experience against future outcome. Overstimulating your nucleus accumbens could lead to uncontrolled overindulgence or even addiction. Discipline and discretion are your primary counterpoints to an overactive reward center.

Both its reaction to fulfillment and the risk of overstimulation will be discussed in later chapters.

Hippocampus

Your hippocampus is where short-term memories are made, and some of them, if deemed important enough, turn into long-term memories. Memories of investments that tanked or pain that resulted from dealing with untrustworthy financial consultants can flood your hippocampus and lead to mental paralysis when it comes to making new investments. You can combat an overactive hippocampus by feeding it positive memories associated with money and by counteracting negative emotions with logic. There will be lots of suggestions for working with memories stored in your hippocampus in the next few chapters, and in the meditation chapter.

Mirror Neurons

Your brain has mirror neurons that effectively reflect the people around you. Whether these people are positive, confident, and energetic, or negative, fearful, and timid, your brain will respond in kind. You can increase your ability to earn more money by choosing work environments and coworkers that stimulate your creativity and nourish your brain.

Brodmann's Area 10 (Frontal-polar Cortex, a.k.a. frontal pole or Area 10)

This area of the human brain is twice as large as it is in great apes and nearly four times more densely packed with neurons. It is also more finely interconnected with the rest of the brain in humans than in great apes; like your ACC spindle cells, its evolution exploded in the last 200,000 years.

Prominent Caltech researchers in the area of social and economic decision-making Drs. James Woodman and John Allman concluded that the sudden expansion of this area may allow for the very human capacity to make good moral and evaluative judgments. They believe that Area 10 (along with ACC spindle cells) is involved in producing the phenomenon we know as intuition, which they theorize is a form of decision biasing based on what we feel is "implicit" knowledge. In a neural sense, that means that Area

10 registers information that arises from our limbic centers as "intuition" and evaluates the information in the PFC for incorporation into our decision processes.

Your Area 10 is located in the same neural neighborhood as your PFC and all its various subdivisions, one of the main regions in the brain where we evaluate the gains we actually receive against what we hoped to receive.

Parietal Cortex

Your parietal cortex processes numerical and verbal information that it then relays to your PFC for further evaluation. Some of the basic arithmetic and math skills needed for good financial decision-making are found here, so it's best not to neglect it!

TIME TO GET TO WORK

Now that we've introduced you to your brain and its unique capabilities—and its blind spots and limitations—let's get out of the gate by discussing how your beliefs play a central role in how your brain functions, and how you can wrestle negative thoughts to the ground and reprogram your thought process to attract greater wealth.

CHAPTER 5

BELIEVE YOU CAN GET RICH

Principle: Your brain believes what you tell it to believe. If you believe in yourself, you can train your brain to play a central role in making your financial dreams come true.

Can you become rich? Not unless you—and your brain—truly believe it's possible. Thinking is what your brain does, and it is strongly influenced by the messages you tell yourself, the actions you undertake, and your worldview. You may be thinking negatively about yourself and your circumstances without even realizing it. In this chapter, you'll learn about this type of automatic negative thinking and the core beliefs that often generate these negative thoughts. Replacing these sorts of thoughts with positive, or at least neutral, thoughts and actions will change your inner money script to one that primes you to be optimistic and successful.

HOW DO YOU THINK ABOUT MONEY?

Recognizing your automatic thoughts about money, your career, and your goals can go a long way towards identifying what you need to work on most. So let's begin by taking an assessment of how you think about money.

1. **I learned everything I know about money:**
   A. by spending as much as possible.
   B. by making mistakes along the way.
   C. by listening to my parents' advice.
   D. by reading financial books.

2. **When I think about money, I:**
   A. think I need lots more of it.
   B. worry that I don't have enough of it.
   C. think of ways to cut back on my spending.
   D. dream up new ways to make more money.

3. **Thinking about money makes me feel:**
   A. uncertain about how to manage my finances.
   B. sad because I need more of it.
   C. anxious about finding new ways to earn more.
   D. confident that I'll find a way to earn more.

4. **I believe that money is:**
   A. something to enjoy immediately.
   B. always slipping through my fingers, so I never seem to have enough.
   C. something I have to work hard to earn.
   D. only one measurement of my success.

5. **I think of myself as rich:**
   A. when I have enough money for two months' expenses.
   B. when I can go on vacation and eat in fancy restaurants.

C. when I am debt-free and can comfortably pay all my bills.

D. when I am debt-free, pay all my bills on time, and continue to add to my savings account and my investment account.

6. I think being an entrepreneur:

A. would involve far more risk than I'd want to take.

B. would require more money than I'll ever have.

C. would be a lot of fun, if I only had an idea.

D. appeals to me greatly.

7. When I receive my paycheck:

A. I immediately buy that item I have been eyeing for several weeks.

B. I pay some of my bills and then splurge on extras.

C. I pay my bills on time and then treat myself.

D. I pay my bills and then allocate what is remaining into three accounts: savings, investments, and pleasure.

Answer Key

If you chose mostly As, you are skating on thin ice when it comes to financial consciousness. You're more comfortable wearing a blindfold than stepping up to the plate. Your financial decisions are far below your potential, but the good news is that you can make huge strides by reading this book and acting on the advice.

If you chose mostly Bs, your financial consciousness fades in and out. You have some concrete knowledge but continue to make most of your financial decisions on emotionally based assumptions. Once you realize that you can dispel those emotional triggers and take a more realistic appraisal of your situation, you will eagerly take up the sword.

If you chose mostly Cs, you have a reasonable grip on your finances, but you aren't dreaming big enough. You've imposed limitations that are holding you back. It's like you're standing at the gates of financial wealth but are afraid to wrench open the door. Once you believe you can get rich, you'll wrench open that door with gusto.

If you chose mostly Ds, what are you waiting for? You have a strong grip on financial reality laced with a proper dose of visionary faith. You know you can do whatever it takes, but you've been hesitant to spring into action. With a little work on thought pruning, you'll light a fire under yourself that will make all your dreams come true. You are ready to take charge of your financial life.

THE THREE KINDS OF THOUGHTS—AND HOW THEY AFFECT YOUR WEALTH

Your brain interprets the world through three basic patterns of thinking: automatic thoughts, assumptions, and core beliefs. To train your brain to get rich, you need to understand how these thoughts originate, how they can positively or negatively affect how you live your life, how you choose (or don't consciously choose) the actions you take to increase wealth, and how you can develop the type of control over your thinking that trains your brain to help you get rich.

Automatic Thoughts

Automatic thoughts are conscious or unconscious thoughts that you have accepted as true. This often happens without thoughtful analysis. Do any of these sound familiar?

- I don't like my job.
- I can't trust my boss.
- I never have any creative thoughts.

- I'm slow to catch on.
- I'm not particularly good at anything.
- I just can't get excited about learning anything new.
- I find life boring.
- I don't have a head for numbers.

These thoughts can simplify your life by narrowing down what you have to think about, but they can also work against you if they are not true or are self-limiting.

Are You Operating on Automatic Responses?

If you're relying on automatic responses to see you through the day, you may be financially unconscious. You're financially unconscious if you:

- Resist facing your real financial situation.
- Employ defensive strategies, such as denial.
- Allow your unexamined beliefs to influence your financial decisions.
- Don't know what you need to know to make solid financial decisions.
- Aren't using all your brain resources to make sound financial decisions.
- Make decisions solely based on emotions.
- Don't learn from your mistakes.
- Turn over all financial responsibilities to others.

Recognizing when you're on automatic pilot empowers you to take action that will engage your brain's CEO in your decision-making process.

Assumptions

Whether they are conscious or unconscious, negative or fearful, automatic thoughts can cause your body to feel stressed, which causes your brain to release stress-related hormones. The more your brain learns to release stress hormones on a regular basis, the more it's wired to remain on high alert, anticipating danger when none may be present. This creates a cataclysm of hormonal and neuronal changes that can impede your better financial judgment.

You can train your brain to downplay automatic negative thoughts and rewire itself to create more positive forms of self-talk, rewiring your brain to focus on thoughts that support rather than deflate your aspirations. Mindfulness—focusing on what is happening in the present rather than what happened or might happen—is a useful tool for replacing negative automatic thoughts with more positive ones. Mindfulness-based meditation, one of the most effective ways to learn and practice mindfulness, will be explored in depth in Chapter 9.

Assumptions are thoughts that have developed from your life experience or from ideas that have been influenced or imposed by others upon you. As with automatic thoughts, assumptions also serve as a shortcut for your brain to interpret what is happening in your life, or what could happen in your future. Assumptions can be conscious or unconscious thoughts that you created—or your brain interpreted—based on sensory perceptions, what others taught you to believe, and the reaction of your automatic thoughts interacting with your core beliefs to interpret reality.

Assumptions You May Make

- I came up with a great idea, but I know my boss will reject it so I won't say anything.
- I would love to land that promotion, but my boss doesn't think I'm smart enough so I don't want to embarrass myself by asking for the job.

- I would love to be a doctor but I don't think I could make it into medical school.
- My brother has always been the favored son and because I already know that my parents will select him to be the company president, why should I work so hard?

Challenging Your Negative Assumptions

Negative assumptions often lead to unnecessary worrying, feeling fearful in safe situations, and withholding the full expression of your personality. You can get into the habit of assuming the worst, which can essentially paralyze your brain when it comes to finding creative solutions and generating positive action.

Name Your Horse

Instead of riding through life on an unnamed horse, which in this case would be whatever unnamed thoughts are holding you back, conquer your fear by naming the thoughts that set it galloping. The closer you can come to naming what causes your fear of being successful, the more you can demystify it for yourself—and for your brain. Once you name it, you can use your brain's rich resources to find a solution. Sometimes simply bringing negative thoughts to consciousness is enough to reduce their influence; if not, you can address and dispel the fear behind them and create new thoughts that will counteract them.

Challenging the assumptions that may be leading you—and your brain—down negative pathways prepares your brain for the creation of new neuronal pathways. Meditation can help you deflect negative thoughts and replace them with positive thoughts—and to live more fully in the present where you can consciously choose how you think about what's happening rather than rehashing your past to draw the same old conclusions. Creating and using positive affirmations also helps you train your brain to "see" things in a more positive, uplifting light.

Core Beliefs

Core beliefs are broad generalizations about yourself and about how the world works that your brain has accepted as true and that you rely upon to interpret what happens.

Examples of core beliefs that could be negatively affecting your ability to become rich would be:

- Women aren't as smart as men.
- I don't have what it takes to be truly successful.
- You can only be successful through connections.
- Rich people can't be trusted.

Your theories that underlie your core beliefs—even if they are illogical—effectively lock in, or lock down, your thought processes by reinforcing what you already believe. This causes your brain to go down the same old neuronal pathways and to congregate even more synapses that support your existing core beliefs.

Core beliefs wire your brain to respond to new experiences in the same old way—and often it happens so quickly that you don't question it—unless and until something goes terribly wrong in your life, or you have an experience that calls your core beliefs into question. Such an experience could be something positive, such as a high-level job offer or a boss who believes you're the smartest employee she has on staff. When positive events challenge your negative core beliefs, it can throw you—and your brain—into a tizzy. Hopefully, you'll recognize the tizzy as a good thing and use it to challenge your negative assumptions and to replace negative core beliefs with positive core beliefs.

Unfortunately, core beliefs are more deeply ingrained than automatic thoughts and assumptions, and thus are harder to discharge (as in removing the electrical charge that has become accustomed to traveling down the same neuronal pathways). However, working on your automatic thoughts and your assumptions can help you eventually reframe your core beliefs so they become more realistic and positive. You can whittle away negative core beliefs and supplant them with positive core beliefs—and that *will* change your brain and your life.

YOU ARE WHAT YOU THINK

Your thoughts form your character, how you operate in the world, how far you travel mentally, physically, and spiritually. You are what you think you are, and all of your actions proceed from thought. Your inner thoughts will always be reflected in your outer circumstances, because self-generated changes in your life are always preceded by changes in the way you think about something.

The Power of Positive Thoughts

Every thought releases brain chemicals. Being focused on negative thoughts effectively saps the brain of its positive forcefulness, slows it down, and can go as far as dimming your brain's ability to function, even creating depression. On the flip side, thinking positive, happy, hopeful, optimistic, joyful thoughts decreases cortisol and produces serotonin, which creates a sense of well-being. This helps your brain function at peak capacity. Happy thoughts and positive thinking, in general, support brain growth, as well as the generation and reinforcement of new synapses, especially in your PFC.

Why It's Better to Be an Optimist

When it comes to creating wealth, because optimists believe in themselves and their abilities (and good fortune), they tend to have the upper hand. Optimists are generally more confident and more likely to trust their instincts, while pessimists are more likely to doubt their instincts and themselves. In fact, scientists have discovered important differences between the two personalities.

Going over to the Bright Side

When negative thoughts (and fears) threaten to dampen your enthusiasm, it's time to look for the bright side of negative situations. For instance, rather than obsessively focusing on the negative effects of the current economic downturn, try thinking of positive counterpoints, such as:

- More people are living within their means.
- More people are paying down their debt.
- Fewer people are using credit cards to buy things they can't afford.
- People who can't afford a loan aren't being given a loan.
- More people are saving at least 5 percent of their income.
- More people are opening new businesses.
- More people are growing their own food.
- More people are spending time at home with their families.
- More people are focused on quality rather than quantity.
- Anyone with cash to spare, or decades to wait, has great opportunities to invest.

Just thinking these types of positive thoughts will stimulate your brain's PFC in positive ways, generating confidence as opposed to fear. The more you learn to reframe negative thoughts into positive ones, the more your brain will follow your lead.

The Money-Making Traits of Optimists

Optimists attribute good events to themselves in terms of permanence, citing their traits and abilities as the cause, and bad events as transient (using terms such as "sometimes" or "lately" to describe negative events). Their approach to life supports their quest for wealth because it allows them to:

- weather financial ups and downs more easily and more successfully
- see setbacks as surmountable and particular to a single external problem or other people, not themselves
- lead happy, rich, fulfilled lives because they expect to lead happy, rich, fulfilled lives
- spend the least amount of time alone, and the most time socializing and networking, making the connections they need to build wealth
- foster healthier relationships which serve them at work, at home, and in the world at large
- take better care of themselves—and their brains
- live longer and richer than pessimists

The Wealth-Sabotaging Traits of Pessimists

Pessimists, on the other hand, attribute good events not to themselves but to outside forces, such as moods and effort, and bad events as permanent conditions ("always" or "never"). In addition they:

- automatically assume setbacks are permanent, pervasive, and due to personal failings. This does not help them recover easily from financial ups and downs
- are eight times more likely to be depressed than optimists. Depressed people, by definition, are not active, and wealth creation is an active pursuit

- are less successful at school and work, which directly impacts their ability to make a living
- have rockier relationships, which thwarts the efforts needed to make connections, keep a high-paying job, and get rich
- die sooner than optimists—whether they managed to get rich or not

The good news is that you can use your mind to tamp down the negative thoughts that lead to pessimism while ramping up the positive thoughts that lead to optimism. Even if cynicism or pessimism runs in your family, you can change the way your brain functions by setting up neuronal roadblocks and diminishing the neuronal patterns linked to negative thinking. You may not be able to completely erase a genetic tendency toward pessimist thinking, but you have the ability to significantly reduce its impact.

NEGATIVE THINKING, NEGATIVE BALANCE

Negative thinking slows down brain coordination, making it difficult to process thoughts and find solutions. Feeling frightened, which often happens when focused on negative outcomes, has been shown to decrease activity in your cerebellum, which slows the brain's ability to process new information—limiting your ability to practice creative problem solving. Additionally, the fear factor impacts your left temporal lobe, which affects mood, memory, and impulse control.

Your frontal lobe, particularly your PFC, decides what is important according to the amount of attention you pay to something and how you feel about it. Thus, the more you focus on negativity, the more synapses and neurons your brain will create that support your negative thought process.

Your hippocampus provides the context of stored memories, which means the emotional tone and description your mind creates can potentially rewire your brain by creating stronger neuronal pathways and synapses. What you think and feel about a certain situation or thing can become so deeply ingrained that you will have to work hard to dismantle the negative connections and rewire your brain in order to be less afraid, to think positively, to believe that dreams can come true, to trust that your efforts will be successful.

THE ROLE YOUR MOODS PLAY

Your moods can affect your thought processes and how your brain works. When you're feeling positive, you're more likely to seek solutions and take positive action. When you're feeling gloomy, you have a sense of futility and your brain effectively shuts down and becomes resistant to—or incapable of—taking action.

Remember: "Neurons that fire together, wire together." If you feel anxious every time you have to interview for a new job, that will make interviewing for new jobs even harder—anxiety will be married to your thoughts and memories associated with job hunting. Also, the more you feel anxious, the more prone you'll be to anxiety, because your hormonal and chemical reactions will travel down the same neuronal highway, straining rather than quieting your amygdala. In a way, you end up training your brain to be oversensitive and to overreact to normal stresses.

Negative moods aren't all bad. In fact, negative emotions help you realize when you aren't in alignment with your needs and values, when you aren't feeling loved, when your needs aren't being met, and when you are in danger. See those negative feelings as information, a way to fully know how you're feeling about each situation. What is important is for you to be able to distinguish between negative feelings which lead to corrective action and those which serve to undermine your ability to realize your goals, both personally and financially. The more you have a firm grip on scary situations, the more you can tamp down scary feelings and quiet your amygdala, the fearful part of your brain.

Using Negative Thoughts as a Roadmap

When seen as the guideposts they are, negative thoughts can be useful tools on your way to wealth. They provide information about your fears that you can address in a way that resolves them and further nudges you into positive action. Also, negative thought patterns are learned and can be transformed into positive thought patterns, which will rewire your brain to think more positively. Once you identify the negative thoughts that are holding you back, you can tamp down those neural pathways and connections, and create new, more informed, optimistic neural pathways and connections that counteract—and eventually erase—the negative ones.

TECHNIQUES FOR CHANGING YOUR NEGATIVE THOUGHTS

If you are besieged by negative thoughts, or have low self-esteem, or tend to expect the worst to happen in almost any situation, it's important to take the reins and turn the tide. Luckily, you can greatly diminish negative thought patterns using a few simple techniques. We'll discuss a few, such as challenging absolutes, neutralizing negative self-talk, distracting your thoughts, and creating positive affirmations.

With repeated practice, over time, you can literally retrain your brain to think more productively and to expect the best to happen in almost every situation. You're the one in control, the one who can direct your brain to perceive events and experience feelings and create expectations. Get ready to flick off your "auto-pilot" switch and engage your brain in your quest for wealth.

Technique #1: Challenge Absolutes

We all tend to think in absolutes: *If I don't get this done, my boss will fire me.* Or, *If I lose this deal, I'll go broke.* After the fact, when the panic has subsided, you may even laugh about how far you took the paranoia. Still, rather than being funny, this kind of black-and-white catastrophic thinking is unproductive, and it is important to break the pattern. The next time you're in one of those situations, take a second to challenge the absolutes your crafty mind is spinning. Write them down (in black and white) so you can see how narrowly your mind has prescripted the outcome. Nine times out of ten, you've exaggerated the situation and the consequences. Every time you find yourself thinking in black-and-white terms, take the time to make a list of a broad range of conceivable outcomes. This will help your brain provide more creative solutions and to envision the positive outcome you desire.

Technique #2: Neutralize Negative Self-Talk

Many of us are saddled with our own unique brand of negative self-talk: *I'm handling this all wrong. I'm such a screw-up. Everyone is smarter than I am.* If you're someone whose chattering mind serves up a buffet of negative self-talk, it's time to identify and challenge those internal, nagging voices. These thoughts usually pop up when you're attempting to learn something new and an insecure and skeptical voice in your mind starts whispering:

- You don't know how to pitch a new client.
- You're no good at convincing people to try new things.
- You're going to screw up the deal and make everyone mad.

Confront these thoughts directly and recast them by stating more realistic positives:

- I've pitched my ideas to my supervisor and my boss.
- My supervisor and my boss were impressed with my capabilities.
- I am extremely well-prepared and have a good chance of landing this deal.

Do this often enough and you will find that your inner voice becomes more supportive and optimistic.

Ways to Stimulate Positive Thinking

You can activate positive emotions by stimulating the part of your brain (your left PFC) that controls them. Some actions you can take include:

- Label your problems. Your left PFC plays a role in expressing and understanding language, so labeling your problems brings it into play.
- Think positive thoughts. Forcing yourself to see the brighter side of problems can decrease activity in your amygdala (by downplaying the negative emotions) and increase activity in your left PFC, which will help you find solutions.
- Find something to motivate you. Creating an emotional reward will link desire to your need to take action to resolve problems.
- Take positive action. Taking action strengthens neuronal pathways and synapses in your left PFC.

Identifying problems, taking actions to correct them, and identifying the rewards that come from the actions turns negatives into positives and engages your left PFC, quieting the parts of your brain that heighten fear and negativity.

Technique #3: Distract Your Thoughts

If you're someone whose brain is so awash with scattered thoughts that you can't focus, distracting your mind may prove very helpful, particularly when you need to stop obsessing about things you cannot control or change. According to a University of Oregon study, it's fairly impossible to think about more than four things at once, which means you can narrow down the chatter.

It's as simple as this: Go *do* something else, a task that will require you to concentrate solely on it. Create the Power Point presentation your boss needs, make a detailed list of the twenty things you need to handle pronto and the steps you need to take to get each done, or, perhaps better yet, go to the gym for a workout, i.e., *do something* that requires concentration, or do something physical that will completely distract your mind chatter.

We'll discuss additional techniques in Chapter 9, particularly mindfulness, which is a healthy way to take control of your thoughts.

Technique #4: Create Money Mantras

Instead of letting a barrage of negative thoughts dominate your life, create a list of positive thoughts to counter them. Consider these money mantras very specific to each situation and as visually detailed as possible, which will help your brain picture them as if they are already true. Instead of thinking negatively about your situation, whatever it is, use positive affirmations such as:

- "Executing this project is easier than I imagined. I already know everything I need to know."
- "Saving money is easier than I imagined. I've already identified multiple ways I can cut back on expenses."
- "Making cold calls is easier than I imagined. I already have a list of qualified leads who will be happy to buy my product."

Money mantras help you relax your brain, and when your brain is relaxed, it's in a much better position to offer up those ideas and solutions you need to perform at your best.

Repeating these types of mantras multiple times throughout the day will create a mental image of success in your mind that your brain will be happy to fulfill. At the very least, formulating positive affirmations will calm your nerves and set the stage for a happier outcome . . . and then you *will* create your report on time, to your best ability, which will reinforce positive envisioning for the next high-pressure situation, and the next, and so on. Experiment with positive affirmations in different situations, and then sit back to watch how well your brain functions when it's been instructed to create the ideal ending.

Write down your money mantras and keep them with you so the minute you become aware of negativity, you can read the affirmations. This will help your brain drown out the negative thoughts and not only focus on, but affirm, what you want to have happen. It's also helpful to paste your list on your bathroom mirror so that you can see them continually.

TRANSFORMING NEGATIVE THOUGHTS INTO POSITIVE ACTION

One of the best ways to train your brain is to take positive action that reinforces the kind of thinking you want to achieve. Remember Hebb's Law: "Neurons that fire together, wire together." Here are six simple steps you can take to transform your negative thought patterns into positive action:

1. Identify your conscious and unconscious thoughts, particularly negative ones that keep your mind going in nonproductive circles.
2. Defuse these negative thoughts by compiling contradictory evidence.

3. Argue with the part of yourself that believes the negative thoughts.
4. Create a different explanation to refute the original negative thought.
5. Loosen up on being judgmental—of yourself and others.
6. Support positive thoughts with validation and create scenarios where you can re-experience them, as needed.

Basically, you want to work toward the following goals:

- Determine why you are feeling upset and/or thinking and behaving in an unhelpful way that is contrary to your goals.
- Gain insight into why you think the way you do, addressing underlying beliefs about the way you see yourself, others, and your environment that are holding you back.
- Modify your negative thoughts and any unrealistic beliefs that contribute to them.
- Learn to appraise situations and problems more objectively.

Now take your situation, create a list of positive counterpoints, and then purposefully focus on the bright side. This will train your brain to think more positively.

TECHNIQUES FOR TURNING POSITIVE THOUGHTS INTO POSITIVE ACTION

Now that you've worked on training your brain to think positive thoughts, it's time to take it to the next level, i.e., turning those positive thoughts into positive actions. The more you take positive action, the more your brain uses its resources to assist you in transforming your ideas into realities that will help you gain wealth and success. Remember: Your brain is at your service, but it's up to you to use your mind to train your brain to get rich, so let's discuss techniques you can adopt.

Control Your Subconscious

You have control over what your subconscious mind knows about. Information comes in through your senses, but you have an opportunity to use your conscious mind to tell your subconscious mind how to process it. Purposefully choose a positive point of view in all situations.

Focus on the Desired Outcome

Use your powers of concentration to focus on your goal each day. Have a written list of actions you need to take to manifest your goal and read it before you go to bed at night and when you get up in the morning. Post notes around your desk or your bathroom mirror or your refrigerator to engage your mind in the manifestation. Doing so fixates your mind on achieving your desired goal. Any thought that is regularly repeated burrows into your subconscious mind. Eventually, it is accepted and acted upon by your subconscious mind as if it were true.

Visualize the Desired Outcome

Create mental pictures that "trick" your subconscious mind into believing your goal has already been achieved, such as picturing a bank statement that has a $100,000 balance, or better yet how a stack of $1,000 bills will look spread out on your table. Visualizations attached to emotion have more juice, particularly when attached to positive emotions. If you convince your subconscious mind that your dream will manifest, and hold on to that belief despite any twists or turns that make it seem like they may not come true, your subconscious mind will translate your belief into physical action. Your mind has the power to make it true.

Acquire Specialized Knowledge

In order to succeed at any endeavor, you need to learn as much as you can about the industry you're working in and the product or service that you provide. You use that knowledge to make your venture a success. The more time you spend acquiring knowledge, the more your brain will comply by firing existing synapses and creating new synapses related to the accumulation and processing of that knowledge. Making the learning process enjoyable will help wire positive feelings to positive action. Instead of grumbling when you have to study, remind yourself—and your mind—that this process is moving you ever closer to your goal, and then get excited! Your brain will respond accordingly.

Use Your Imagination

Instead of accepting the tried-and-true knowledge, exercise your brain by rearranging concepts, ideas, or plans to create a new way of doing something. This act of creativity spurs even more creativity. The more you concentrate on something, the more ideas your brain will offer up. Get fired up and let your passion for the subject propel your quest. Creative imagination is usually driven by heightened desire or need, which stimulates your mind and helps your brain function at peak capacity. Engage in extracurricular activities that stimulate creativity. Take a painting, writing, or acting class, or anything else that you tend to associate with creativity.

HOW TO TURN THOUGHTS INTO REALITY

Now that you've learned techniques for transforming your thoughts into action, the next step is to turn your newly positive thoughts into a more definitive action plan. Here's what to do:

- Identify your strongest desire.
- Get obsessed and stay obsessed with achieving it.
- Set your sights on the specifics of what you want.
- Doggedly pursue your goal(s).
- When obstacles arise, find ways to overcome them.
- Never give up.

To form neural pathways, you need make conscious efforts to repeatedly reinforce your goals and take positive action. This helps your brain form and begin to favor the new neuronal pathway, as opposed to routinely falling into old, nonproductive ruts. If you don't create supportive brain activity, your lazy brain will take the easy way out.

TENDING YOUR THOUGHTS

Just as a garden must be tended, so must your thoughts. Our thoughts can help us achieve our dreams or succumb to our fears. How stubbornly we hold on to negative thoughts or how doggedly we pursue positive thoughts determines what happens next. To achieve wealth, you'll need to weed out aversive thoughts, prune unwieldy thoughts, plant thought seeds that will lead the way, nourish them as they grow, and be prepared and receptive when it's time to eagerly sow the rewards.

Now that you've weeded your garden and planted some seed thoughts that will blossom into your believing that you can get rich, it's time to turn the page, literally and figuratively, to focus on creating your intention to get rich.

CHAPTER 6

CREATE THE INTENTION TO GET RICH

Principle: Defining your values and your true intention helps your brain focus, support, monitor, and reward the completion of goals that support your quest for success.

When an interviewer asked a rags-to-riches wealthy industrialist and philanthropist, "What steps did you take in becoming successful?" the industrialist responded, "That's not the first question to ask. The first question to ask is, 'Why did I want to be successful?'"

Why is a question many of us forget to ask, especially of ourselves. To launch your journey to wealth, the major questions you want to ask yourself are:

- Why do I want financial wealth?
- What will being rich mean to me?

The answers to these two questions will help you begin the process of creating intentions. As you'll recall from Chapters 3 and 4, your brain will believe whatever you tell it to believe. As such, creating intentions specific to your quest for wealth will create powerful roadmaps for your brain to follow.

TRUE INTENTIONS

As discussed in previous chapters, if you envision something hard enough, your brain will believe that it's already happened. That means that the creation and reinforcement of intentions is a powerful and effective method for creating the neural pathways you need to get rich. As such, it's extremely important that you create intentions that resonate on every level with your truest desires. The following quiz will help you begin the process.

The *Do I Know My True Intentions?* Quiz

1. **I really want to be rich because:**
   - **A.** I could buy whatever I wanted.
   - **B.** I could send my children to college.
   - **C.** I want security for my family and inheritances for my children.
   - **D.** having a lot of money would allow me to start a new business.

2. **When it comes to setting financial or professional goals, I:**
   - **A.** don't think long-term . . . I don't even think short-term.
   - **B.** have a vague idea of what I want out of life.
   - **C.** have a few major goals, but no real game plan to achieve them.
   - **D.** make it a habit to set short- and long-term goals and review them every six months.

3. **The best thing that having goals does for me is:**
   - **A.** they leave me feeling guilty when I don't achieve them.
   - **B.** they help me figure out what I want to happen next.
   - **C.** they are a way to establish priorities.
   - **D.** they keep me focused and proactive.

4. **A typical financial goal for me would be:**
   A. stop spending so much money eating in restaurants.
   B. cut back on expenses and save $250 a month.
   C. stick to a detailed budget and save 10 percent of my income this year.
   D. create a business plan and launch my new business by the end of the year.

5. **A typical career goal for me would be:**
   A. improve my relationship with my boss.
   B. go to night school to improve my skills.
   C. send out resumes to find a new job that's one rung up the ladder.
   D. figure out who I want to work for and target the job I want.

6. **When I accomplish a goal, I:**
   A. feel pretty good for about ten minutes.
   B. check it off my list and move on to the next one.
   C. give myself a pat on the back.
   D. celebrate my accomplishment by doing something fun.

Answer Key

If you chose mostly As, you need a long talk with yourself to figure out what you want out of life and how to get it. Once you know your true intentions and create achievable goals that will help you create the wealth that's right for you, you can power forward with your life.

If you chose mostly Bs, you are making some effort to figure out what you want career-wise, but you haven't put the full force of your brainpower to work. Your brain stands ready to be an amazing ally, and this chapter will offer you great ideas for marshaling its forces and putting it to work for you.

If you chose mostly Cs, you have been making marginal progress, but you aren't mobilizing your brain's amazing ability to handle complex thinking. When you put in some hard time figuring out concrete goals and a plan to achieve them, you'll be unstoppable.

If you chose mostly Ds, you already understand the importance of knowing what you want, why you want it, and what you have to do to get it. Still, there's a lot you can do to take full advantage of your brain's assets. With a little work, you'll be even more unstoppable.

IDENTIFY YOUR PASSIONS

Success doesn't typically come from latching onto opportunities willy-nilly. Success usually results from digging deep within yourself to identify what matters most to you, what you want to do with this precious life you have been given, and how much time and energy you are willing to invest to make your dreams come true. Identifying those passions and your life purpose helps you focus on what's truly important, seek and find the opportunities that will lead to success, and invest more energy in your pursuits. If you love what you do, it will open the floodgates, unleash your potential, and make you more expansive, more creative, more productive—and more successful.

Once you determine the whys in your life—*why do I love geography with a passion, why does the prospect of traveling the world excite me, why do I enjoy finding new ways of doing things, why do I feel this need to explore and map new territory*, and so on—then determining your true intention, what you want to do with your life, will come easily. It will be right there in your answers.

In the above example, the person thinking these thoughts will probably be happiest if she works for the government or a business that uses her skills and passions in the field, traveling the globe, going where no one has gone before, mapping new territory. The intention in this case might be to live a life spent traveling the world, gaining a sense of identity and purpose by exploring regions that few people have visited. The manifestations could lead to surprises, such as an interest in marketing exotic oils from India or leading a charity that will teach modern skills to impoverished tribes in Africa, but none of that is likely to happen if the person had not first identified her life intention.

Intend to Make Money

Researchers working under Richard Davidson at the University of Wisconsin measured what happens in the brains of Tibetan monks when they envision themselves performing compassionate acts. Admittedly, Tibetan monks spend most of their time meditating, and they are considered masters of intention. Still it came as a bit of shock when their brain scans revealed that merely envisioning their future behavior dramatically increased activity in two areas of the monks' brains: the prefrontal cortex, which flooded them with a sense of well-being, and the areas involved with motor planning, as if they were preparing to leap into action.

Create Your Mission Statement

What you need is a mission statement for your life, something that conveys who you are, what you value most, and what you want to accomplish. Think big in defining your intentions—and your values and goals—but keep reviewing, polishing, and refining them until you have something you can print on a 4" x 6" index card and tape to your bathroom mirror, and your refrigerator, and your dashboard, and wherever else you happen to look daily. Intentions are not written in stone, and they may indeed change as you live life and grow as a person, but knowing your intentions—for right now, for next month, for next year, and for your life—focuses all your brain's resources so it can help you discover and maximize pathways to success.

Defining your intention for your life will quite naturally lead to mapping out your career path. It doesn't take a neuroscientist to tell you that having a clear, well-defined intention adds tremendous heft to purpose, meaning, and motivation. It's hard to take that next step towards financial wealth if you don't have a clue what will ultimately bring you the greatest happiness and fulfillment. If you know that, you're already taking your first steps on the path to wealth.

Interestingly, in the Buddhist tradition, wise intention is the second step on the eightfold path to the relief of suffering, i.e., happiness. To Buddhists, emotions and motivation lead to intention and intention precedes action. Nothing happens without intention. All things are first created in the mind and then created in the environment. *Every* thought is truly an intention—something your brain already knows.

Clarify Your Intention to Make Money

Your brain also already knows that your intentions and *authentic* desires create your world. Your intentions are your high ideals and motivate you to reach for specific goals. Most people don't seek goals like finding a new relationship, earning more money, or creating a fit body simply for the sake of having those things in and of themselves. They are motivated because of what they believe they will experience by having a new body, a new relationship, or more money in their lives. In other words, you are driven toward achievement goals by the desire (intention) to be peaceful, grateful, joyous, loving, fulfilled, loved, healthy, or financially secure. By starting with your intentions, you get right to the source of what you truly want. Intentions are the core and the magic of all your values, goals, and desires.

Intentions and Your Quest for Wealth

Therefore, bringing your intentions to consciousness by meditation (which we'll discuss in Chapter 9) or any other method of interior observation and reflection empowers you. It helps you override unexamined assumptions and habits of thinking that may be thwarting your efforts to generate wealth. Once you bring your intentions to consciousness, you will gain a deeper sense of purpose and clarity.

Intentions are very important in your quest for wealth because they:

- allow your brain to focus on money
- narrow down the field of awareness, which helps your brain direct its energy towards building wealth
- increase self-awareness and perception of what's going on in your mind
- help you stay in the now, focused on what needs to happen to improve your finances
- help you reflect on what's working and not working
- let you see and address any possible resistance to making money.

But this is mostly how intentions affect your mind; let's now discuss how they specifically affect your brain.

PAY ATTENTION TO WEALTH

Your brain's reticular cortex directs incoming stimuli to your conscious or unconscious mind, serving as a sort of gatekeeper, allowing you to tune in to whatever you decide is important and requires attention and tune out what you decide is unimportant and not worthy of attention. Understanding this process helps ensure that you are paying attention to the right things—in this case, the things that will help you build wealth.

To fire up your reticular cortex and thereby make sure information (stimuli) gets sorted correctly, focus on what you want. Be as specific as you can. Know what you want and why you want it. In narrowing your focus, you will engage your reticular cortex in blocking excess thoughts and distracting sensations, which will help you move beyond wishful thinking and into manifestation of your intentions.

What Motivates You?

Desiring financial success isn't solely about the amount of greenbacks you tally up; it's also about achievement, pride, power, control, security, ownership, and freedom, to name a few motivational aspirations. Any emotions or thoughts you have about money can be extremely complex as they are affected by a multitude of ideas or feelings stemming from your family history, your personal history, and the larger culture. To help your brain work hard to make you rich, you need to identify and focus on what motivates you. Doing so will help your brain call upon those motivations when important decisions or challenges arise.

Think of it as developing a mind that embraces abundance and prosperity. When you've identified an intention, focused on it, and made a clear, committed decision to act upon your intention, your mind will open the universal floodgates, bringing you all the resources you need, sometimes in seemingly mysterious or impossible ways.

Unite Your Money Consciousness

If your consciousness is divided against itself, it's practically impossible for your mind to be able to manifest your desires. A wishy-washy intention and a blurry lens don't motivate your subconscious to offer up all the energy and creativity you'll need to make it happen. One essential component of learning to use your consciousness to create what you desire is remaining consistent in your thinking. When you are consistent in your thoughts, your goal will manifest with ease. But when you have wildly inconsistent thoughts about what you want in life, your energies will be too dissipated, and you will end up frustrated and disappointed. To train your brain to work with you on manifesting your intentions, you need to clear the path, sharpen your focus, and get your mental ducks in a row.

To achieve your dreams, you need to clarify your intentions and then take actions that support those intentions. Creating goals is an ideal way to formulate and accomplish actions that will propel you closer to achieving your intention of becoming financially secure by making a lot more money.

UNDERSTAND YOUR VALUES

Your brain requires great clarity so, in addition to defining your life purpose and intentions, take time to specifically identify your values. That is the next step to creating achievable goals.

Values are your spiritual bottom line—what will ultimately bring you meaningful pleasure. Your values define how you happily spend your time.

Values Differ

Money does not have the same meaning and purpose for everyone. You may value service over money, or teaching young souls over being CEO of a major corporation, or the freedom that being an entrepreneur provides over making a killing in the stock market. If you value hard work, you're probably already doing something that requires hard work. If you value connecting with nature, you may already be a nature photographer or a gardener or a vintner. If what you are doing is already in alignment with your values and your life purpose, then you've got a leg up on millions of people who haven't yet brought their values and goals to the forefront of their consciousness and taken action to live a life that supports, nourishes, and expands those values and purposes.

Be Specific and Prolific

Pablo Picasso, one of the most successful and prolific artists of all time, once said, "Our goals can only be reached through the vehicle of a plan, in which we must fervently believe, and upon which we must vigorously act. There is no other route to success." Picasso's philosophy provides an excellent role model for generating success.

The wealthiest people are those who know themselves and their values very well and who feel fulfilled in their work. It's one reason they love to work so hard and why their passion leads them to innovation and experimentation and manifestation. Coming up with ways to turn your passion into financial wealth is like a big fat bonus and something that will flow much easier once your values are in alignment with how you are living your life.

Identify Your Values

Quickly, without overthinking, make a list of your values. Write down as many as you can possibly think of, and then keep polishing and refining the list until you have identified at least five core values that you know in your heart need to play a huge role in how you live your life, and thus how you make your living. It is possible to work outside your values, but you run the risk of never being fully integrated and happy.

Once you have your life mission statement (defined by your intentions) and your five core values, it's time to turn those building blocks into concrete, achievable goals.

CREATE GOALS

If you never create goals, you're far more likely to be haunted by unanswered questions and regrets. Some part of you will always wonder what you might have accomplished if you had taken the time to identify what you really wanted to do, in alignment with your values, and established a game plan for making it happen. Failing to create goals means that you run a high risk of never reaching your full potential or living the life you deserve—or the life that will leave you feeling as if you've made your mark on the world.

Goals are a means to an end, a roadmap you can follow to achieve your dreams. Goals give you a visible point on the horizon that you can march toward. Creating goals that honor your values and your life purpose (or immediate intention) harnesses your energy and focuses it upon making things happen. If successful, long-term goals are a manifestation of your dreams and life purpose; short-term goals provide a step-by-step blueprint.

To help your brain function at its peak capacity in your quest for wealth, it's important to create very clear goals and objectives. Knowing precisely what you want and when you want it to happen delivers clear intention to your brain and fires up the neurons related to the task. There are certain steps you can take to create the types of goals that will vastly improve your chances of success, so let's go through them, one by one.

Be Proactive

Always create positive goals, or at least frame them in a positive way. For example, instead of saying, "I want to stop making blind decisions and panicking when the stock market dips a few points," formulate your goal this way, "I will spend ten minutes a day researching my investments so I feel more comfortable assessing minor market fluctuations." You want your goals to inspire you to make changes that benefit your finances, not punish you for what you perceive as weaknesses. Besides, giving your brain positive thoughts makes it easier for it to function. Giving it negative thoughts, such as to avoid panic selling, makes it so focused on *not doing* something that it misses opportunities *to do* something really positive.

Make Your Goals Meaningful

Studies have consistently shown that people achieve greater life satisfaction when they work for things, or experiences that they value rather than merely for things that bring immediate short-term pleasure. Consciously choosing activities that support your individual (and meaningful) goals creates positive subjective experiences that lead to happiness. Chasing hedonistic goals tends to limit meaningful personal experiences and will do little to make you happy in the long run.

When you give your mind a "don't" message, that is the message that sticks. For example, if you're told "Don't think about that pink elephant," what is the image that immediately pops into your mind? Of course . . . the pink elephant. When a basketball player is poised at the free throw line at a critical juncture of the game, the message being transmitted to his brain had better be "I will make that shot," not "I don't want to miss the basket." A simple flip in the way you word your goals can make all the difference.

If They Can Do It, So Can You

According to Thomas J. Stanley, PhD, author of *Millionaire Women Next Door*, two-thirds of self-made millionaire women regularly set clearly defined goals. In fact, most set daily, weekly, monthly, annual, and lifetime goals. These women also had a history of reaching these goals and their past success served as a motivational tool for additional success. Their success partially lay in their realization that they needed to break down the larger goal into smaller baby steps, and create a hierarchy in the form of daily goals, weekly goals, monthly goals, and finally yearly goals. Creating goals that offer your brain sequential steps helps make the possibility of success more readily attainable. Also, as far as your brain is concerned, each success—no matter how small—registers as a successful experience and triggers the development of neuronal connections that support additional achievement.

Be Specific and Actionable

Your brain will work miracles for you—if it knows what you're asking it to do. When you create goals, be very specific about what it is that you want to achieve. Rather than saying "I want to increase my business," say "I want to develop a new sales strategy based on incentives that will inspire my sales staff to find ten new customers a week. What I need are ideas for incentives that will work and that won't increase my expenses more than 5 percent." Instead of saying "I have just got to learn how to invest my money" (and likely feeling inadequate to the task), say instead "I'm going to understand the three most important rules about investing" (which feels far more achievable). You want to engage your brilliant brain in helping you create greater wealth.

Create a Timeline

Having goals in mind without an action-plan timeline is little more than having ideas floating around in your brain with no direction and no harbor in sight. When you create the goal, create a timeline for achievement. "I want to come up with three ideas for my new product line by next Thursday." Or, "I will spend thirty minutes every morning focused solely on developing new products, and at the end of two weeks, I will choose three that seem most promising and ask for feedback from my coworkers." Studies have shown that knowing when and where you'll take action toward achieving a goal doubles, or even triples, your chances of success.

Be a Realist

As the old saying goes, "Nothing that's worth having comes cheap." Realize right from the start that achieving goals takes time and can involve a lot of preparatory and even seemingly redundant work. Having unrealistic expectations or expecting everything to occur magically sets you up for failure. When you create your goals, take time to break them down into the readily achievable elements that will be required. Assign each a timeline. Also, anticipate possible setbacks and develop ideas for how to overcome obstacles. This is not negative thinking but rather scenario planning. It's arming yourself with reality so you and your brain won't feel surprised or defeated when those inevitable setbacks occur.

Monitor Your Progress

To elicit your brain's help in generating ideas, hold it accountable. Giving it a deadline offers you the opportunity to stay on top of what's occurring. Recording that progress, whether you make a list or keep a journal or simply jot ideas down on your calendar, will keep your brain on high alert. For example, if you set a deadline of two weeks to come up with three new ideas, then having a system by which you monitor your progress will keep your brain constantly searching for ideas. Set aside time each day to record any thoughts related to your goal and your brain will work even harder to serve up more.

Have You Rewarded Your Brain Today?

Reward your brain by keeping it agile through healthy food and exercise. In Chapter 13, we spell out the types of healthy food choices and brainpower boosters that will nourish your brain. For exercise, choose activities that get your heart pumping so that oxygen and blood are flowing to your brain. Sex is great exercise, and choosing sports or other physical activities that are also playful is doubly rewarding. Listening to music, reading your favorite novel, playing the piano, calling a friend to chat, or walking your dog also reward your brain. The goal is to do something that feels good but doesn't put your brain to sleep, the way watching TV would do. Choose something soothing and nourishing to your brain, and for greater benefit, make it something that stimulates a region of your brain that isn't flexed at work.

Pay Attention to Your Brain

Once you've called your brain to attention, it's important to stay alert for any signs that it's on the job. Notice and write down any ideas that surface. Pay attention to what's happening around you because your brain (and your subconscious) will offer up pearls in settings you never expected. Remember, once you've put it on alert, your brain notices things in your environment that pertain to the task, and it will begin to link up memories, perceptions, and ideas. It's your job to notice what happens. Even if you come up empty-handed when the two-week deadline arrives, don't berate yourself— or your brain. Recognize (and even say aloud) that it tried its best and you're confident new ideas are percolating and will spring forth soon. You can also recognize your brain's accomplishments by creating a list of things that you did accomplish, or habits that you started that will make you more prepared for the next goal. Then, keep doing what you were doing to reach the goal, or come up with a new strategy.

The more success you experience in this process of goal setting and achievement, the more it will become second nature for your brain. Knowing how to create success and how to recognize and reward success will train your brain to perform brilliantly.

WHERE'S YOUR FOCUS?

To get rich, you need to focus on the right things to maximize opportunities and avoid mistakes. Here are a few examples of how focus can affect an entrepreneur who owns a business in her quest for wealth:

- If she focuses on productivity, her brain will offer up ways for her to improve productivity, motivate her employees in new ways, and come up with new product lines. Her brain will learn to be constantly searching for innovative ways for her to improve productivity and to inspire and motivate her employees.
- If she focuses on her employees, her brain will assist her in developing leadership skills that will keep her attuned to what's important to them and how she can best serve them.

- If she focuses on innovation, her brain will offer up new ways to look at situations, develop her ability to think outside the box, and generate visionary ideas.

Focus on Saving Rather Than Spending

Until recently, some 59 percent of Americans were focused on spending rather than saving. The recession has led many to reverse the trend and focus on lowering their credit card debt and living within realistic budgets based on income, rather than living beyond their means. Research has consistently shown that savers develop and reinforce healthy financial habits, like budgeting, tracking expenses, balancing their checkbooks monthly, paying bills when they arrive, and living within or below their means. Savers also report feeling confident and happy, while spenders report feeling frustrated and unhappy with their circumstances. Time to go with the positive flow and become a conscientious saver.

So what are *you* focused on that relates to achieving the level of success and wealth you want? Have you been focused on the wrong things? If so, it's essential that you work through the steps outlined in this chapter, focusing you and your brain on what you really want to achieve and/or what you need to focus on to generate the type of success you want to achieve.

Focusing on Short-Term Goals

Short-term goals are extremely important for achieving wealth. They are far more action oriented and not as all-inclusive as long-term goals, which make them far easier to achieve. Short-term goals provide your brain with a clear roadmap of where you want it to focus in the foreseeable future. To maximize their effectiveness, follow these simple guidelines when creating short-term goals:

- **Make them very specific:** Break them down into their smallest denominator. For example: Balance your checkbook every month. Prepare your budget for the household for one month and then confirm if you lived within your budget at the end of that month.
- **Make them measurable:** You should be able to measure results that occur within a certain time frame. For example: Obtain and review your personal credit report and credit score by the end of the next month.
- **Make them attainable:** A good goal is a bit of a stretch, but something you can feel pleased about once you fulfill it. For example: You met your budget last month. You increased your credit score by 10 percent from the end of the year.
- **Make them valuable:** Short-term goals, like long-term goals, should be in alignment with your core values and intentions. For example: You can't grow your wealth if you don't know where the money is coming from and where it goes each month. Teaching yourself financial discipline is essential if you are to become (and stay!) rich.
- **Make them progressive:** Your short-term goals should bring you a step closer to achieving your long-term goals. For example: Learn ten new investment words every month. Increase your savings by 10 percent by the end of the year.
- **Make them primary:** Your goal should stay at the top of your to-do list until it is achieved.

Why Your Brain Loves Short-Term Goals

Short-term goals are not the same as a daily to-do task list. Tasks are steps you take to reach short-term goals, whereas short-term goals are a bar you set for yourself (and your brain) that achieves something of value to you, something that moves you closer to your life purpose—and greater wealth.

Save Your Insula!

Why do some people seem to be naturally adept at saving, and others seem to find more pleasure in spending their cash immediately? Our brains may make the difference. A study published in the *Journal of Consumer Research* showed that when study participants pretended to make buying decisions, activity occurred in an area of the brain called the insula. The insula is usually stimulated when you experience something unpleasant; thus, when it comes to money, insula stimulation can stop your spending, as the act of spending will make you feel uncomfortable. The study concluded that people who have more insula activity in their brains when thinking about spending money are more likely to be savers, and those with less tend to be spenders—that, basically, savers feel a rush when *not* spending because it provides relief from insula activation. Regardless of insula activation, "gut feelings" about money can be overridden by using other parts of your brain, like your PFC, to make financial decisions.

Your brain loves short-term goals because they are easy to comprehend and because they tell it what you want it to focus on each day. That's why having and reviewing a list of short-term goals, and the tasks required to meet them, works so brilliantly. Your brain will be your taskmaster, but it's up to you to create the tasks that matter and to keep your brain alert and focused on achieving them.

Do You Have True Grit?

According to Heidi Grant Halvorson, motivational psychologist and author of *Succeed: How We Can Reach Our Goals*, grit is a willingness to commit to long-term goals, especially in the face of extreme difficulty. She cites studies showing that people with grit obtain more education and achieve higher grades, and notes that grit is what drives certain people to go for the gold, whether it's Olympic gold or winning a spelling bee. The recent movie *True Grit* portrayed the dogged determination of a fourteen-year-old girl who had remarkably clear goals, a driving passion, and unnerving courage. Like most with true grit, she never doubted her ability to achieve her goal, stayed completely focused, and simply refused to give up. If you haven't had true grit up to now, it's never too late to recognize it within yourself and call it forth.

WHY IMMEDIATE GRATIFICATION DEFEATS YOUR PURPOSE

In setting goals, as in living life, you will be constantly facing the choice between immediate and delayed gratification. When faced with a choice between a small, immediate reward ($5 immediately) and a larger reward that would come after a delay ($10 after two hours of waiting), research has shown that people will most often choose the smaller, immediate reward over the larger, later reward. This tendency is called "discounting" by neuroscientists, and it seems to be based both on the expected time delay of reward and the context of the reward. Further, it seems that your brain is using two very different systems in order to compare the two options and make a decision.

The laboratory of Dr. Jonathan Cohen at Princeton has found using fMRI that choosing an immediate reward lights up your limbic "pleasure" centers and may cause a rush of feel-good dopamine that can be hard to fight. However, people who choose the larger, longer-term reward show activation in their PFC and posterior parietal cortex (which is activated when comparing numbers). These people had controlled their emotional centers in favor of making rational financial decisions—and they were the richer for it!

This research finding reveals the importance of delayed gratification and the importance of your PFC in considering the real value of a decision. The ability to delay gratification plays a critical role in wealth creation. Ask any successful entrepreneur how he/she felt when they started their companies and all will report feeling very apprehensive and worried. However, they were able to delay gratification and stay focused for considerable periods of time until their companies became very successful and they could realize their financial goals. They were not looking for get-rich-quick schemes. They relied on the strength of discipline and reason over immediate pleasure to realize their intentions.

HOW YOUR BRAIN BENEFITS FROM INTENTION AND GOAL SETTING

Instead of wasting your brainpower by not being intentionally focused, train your brain to operate at peak capacity by training it to be on the lookout for ways to maximize opportunities to get ever closer to your dreams. The more you train your brain to focus on your intentions and goals, the more it will rise up to the challenge. Here's how your brain can benefit from establishing clear intentions and setting goals:

- Intention gives your brain mental images that it accepts as true, making it easier to create the desired outcome in real time. Intention also wakes up "sleeping neurons" and strengthens and increases the firing of neuronal synapses.
- Intention leads to setting goals, which focuses your brain and keeps all the necessary neurons firing and forging new connections in support of those goals.

- Monitoring intention keeps your brain focused on the task, even while it sleeps!
- Rewarding intention reinforces growth and development of neuronal pathways, and it stimulates your amygdala, in a good way, by linking pleasure to goal achievement.

If you train your brain to excel or to extend service, your brain will become accustomed to finding and reinforcing those types of opportunities. If you train your brain to focus on what is working instead, focusing on problems, it will begin to notice far more positives than negatives.

Clearly identifying intention and focusing on the good things happening in your life will bring them to your brain's full attention, and it will return the favor in spades, offering up ways for you to be happier and wealthier—all you have to do is ask.

TIME TO FOCUS ON LEARNING!

Now that you've identified and clarified your intentions and created goals that will support and foster their achievement, it's time to discuss specific ways you can teach your brain to make solid financial decisions.

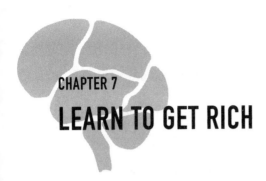

CHAPTER 7
LEARN TO GET RICH

Principle: Your brain is still evolving and often responds in primitive ways to modern problems, which means you need to outsmart it.

Your brain is a marvel, and a marvelous tool you can use on your path to financial success. However, your brain also has odd ways of working and somewhat antiquated wiring that can create obstacles in your path. To succeed financially, you need to understand that your brain's natural way of functioning may present challenges to your goal of getting rich, and you need to understand what you can do to overcome them.

DON'T PUSH THE PANIC BUTTON

One saboteur to getting rich is having a panic button, which stems from an overactive amygdala. If you push the panic button too often, or when making a crucial decision, it can thwart your efforts to gain wealth. To begin, let's assess your comfort level when it comes to financial risk.

1. **I get my news about the stock market from:**
   - **A.** the ticker that's always running at the bottom of my computer screen.
   - **B.** online news so I can see how it's doing three or four times a day.
   - **C.** the nightly news.
   - **D.** the financial section of several newspapers or magazines.

2. **When I purchase a stock, I:**
   - **A.** don't have a clue what I'm doing.
   - **B.** trust my investment counselor to tell me what to buy.
   - **C.** go with my gut instincts.
   - **D.** research the company's financials.

3. **I am comfortable taking risks when:**
   - **A.** the odds are in my favor.
   - **B.** I don't have a lot of money on the line.
   - **C.** it's a calculated risk.
   - **D.** I've balanced the risk with other sources of income that are more stable.

4. **When everyone is panicking about a sharp drop in the stock market, I:**
   - **A.** panic right along with them.
   - **B.** turn off the news.
   - **C.** check several news sources to see if there's a reason for the sharp decline.
   - **D.** check to see if it's really a sharp drop, or only a 1–2 percent drop in the total market.

5. **When a stock I own drops 10 percent, I:**
   A. sell it off immediately.
   B. look to see how the whole market did that day, and then sell if it's down in general.
   C. compare how the stock has performed over the last two years and hold off if it typically rebounds.
   D. evaluate the company's long-term growth, assets, and profitability, and if it's solid, I may wait it out—or sell 25 percent of my holdings to move to a better performing stock.

6. **I rebalance my stock portfolio:**
   A. I don't have a stock portfolio.
   B. I let my company's benefits manager handle my portfolio.
   C. every six months, or whenever the stock market shoots up or down.
   D. once a year for growth-oriented stocks; once every five years for long-term investments.

Answer Key

If you picked mostly As, your brain is saturated with fear and reacts impulsively. It's not your brain's fault because you're the one who's been riling it up. You'll benefit from the wakeup call this chapter provides, one that will calm your brain and help you make more rational decisions.

If you picked mostly Bs, you're also excitable and prone to herd mentality. You need to give your brain a rest occasionally and learn ways to modulate your decisions. With a few tweaks, your brain will once again become your ally.

If you picked mostly Cs, your brain is occasionally firing on all burners, but you'll make even smarter decisions when you understand what needs to be strengthened—and how you can easily do it. Your brain stands ready to serve.

If you picked mostly Ds, you know how to treat your brain right, and it's likely serving up the goodies—in the form of money. However, you can also benefit from a minor tune-up and a few more irons in the fire.

PROBLEM AREAS IN YOUR BRAIN

If your brain is such a great tool, how can it make such lousy decisions sometimes? That's because your brain—which dealt just fine with primitive problems—can't always keep up with the enormous complexity of contemporary society. It still expects threats to come with large teeth and its idea of an excellent coping strategy is to run away—or to hit things really hard. Not surprisingly, these strategies aren't always the best way to build wealth. So, let's look at how your brain's old technology can make it hard to deal with the world's new technology.

- Your more primal, instinctual brain can overpower your more highly developed, reflective brain, leading you to make hasty decisions based on heightened emotions.
- Your brain always seeks to reach decisions in the easiest way possible—with the least emotional and cognitive cost. The tendency to also seek rapid closure can prevent your brain from incorporating new important information that should be considered when making financial decisions.
- Your brain is obsessed with patterns and will spin its wheels searching for them, even when none exist or when they aren't relevant. It can also attach too much value to patterns, such as interpreting the slightest financial trend as a permanent reality.
- Your brain's predilection for tree-search processing—endlessly following thought streams to collect all conceivable data—

means you can literally get lost in thought and fail to take action.

- Your brain is highly susceptible to fear, excitement, and other emotions that can be induced by manipulation, framing (how you or someone you rely on interprets what's happening), and by words that instantly evoke emotion. Emotions can override all reason. That means if, for example, you are faced with negative financial information (a downturn in the stock market), your brain may start to focus on the fear the information creates rather than carefully considering the facts and making a plan to deal with them.

- Your brain seeks certainty, and thus is naturally risk averse. However, to reap financial rewards you often must take risks.

- Your brain can become set in its ways and respond rigidly to new situations.

- Your brain can be so narrowly focused that it misses the big picture.

- Your brain can become addicted to immediate rewards and rank the pursuit of the rewards (even the wrong rewards) above other, more important needs. This is why alcoholism or drug addictions can destroy someone's career.

- Your brain can create and remain susceptible to visual, auditory, and emotional associations, whether or not they have any basis in fact or relevancy to a new situation. Your brain can be highly sensitive to what people around you are thinking or feeling, which leaves you vulnerable to group pressure, even when whatever they are choosing to do might not be in your best interest. Some of this occurs below the level of consciousness.

Now that you have a better understanding of the ways in which your brain can actually work against you, you're ready to learn methods to train your brain to work for you and what you hope to accomplish.

The Good News!

Your neocortical brain *has* evolved over the last 200,000 years—and it continues to evolve—to meet the challenges you need to overcome to survive and thrive. Your brain is adaptable and you have the power to direct your thoughts and even teach it how you want it to process thoughts. Remember: Your brain works for you!

YOUR TWO BRAINS

Okay, you don't really have two brains, but the human brain does have two ways of processing information, which, for the sake of clarity, we'll call "your two brains."

Your Instinctual Brain

This is the more primitive and purely instinctual or *reflexive* part of your brain, specifically, your basal ganglia and limbic system (amygdala and nucleus accumbens). Your reflexive brain (not to be confused with your reflective brain!) receives external and internal sensory information and reacts instinctively to protect you from harm. It is precisely the reflexive function of the brain that results in the survival of the species as it responds immediately to threatening stimuli (e.g., those large teeth) and forms the basis of the fight-or-flight response to danger. The following are some important characteristics of your instinctual brain:

- It receives and relays messages from your environment, and forms your initial "impression" of things that are happening moment-to-moment.
- It is focused primarily on looking for things that will keep you alive, safe, and secure. In this vein, it is focused on avoiding

risky situations and looking for rewarding situations that provide for these goals.

- It is subjective or feeling based.
- It doesn't like uncertainty, and will reframe problems until it can easily understand and address them. Tends toward black-and-white or all-or-nothing thinking.

Your Insightful Brain

The more highly developed region of your brain, specifically your PFC and its associated areas (also known as your *reflective* brain) receives and processes information from your instinctual, reflexive brain, searches your memory database for additional information, links to relevant memories, attributes value and urgency to each situation, and, if it has time, evaluates possibilities and probabilities before making decisions about what must be done.

The following are some important characteristics of your insightful brain:

- It receives and processes messages from your instinctual, reflexive brain, and then searches your memory "database" for connections that it uses to evaluate and rank the new information in terms of relevancy or urgency.
- It is focused on complex and analytical thinking.
- It is involved in forecasting and making plans for your future.
- It is largely objective or factually based.
- It reacts to numbers and words.

Why You Have to Take Control

Long ago, before modern civilization, humans, like animals, relied primarily on their instinctual or reflexive functioning of their brains. They used their brains to process sensory information, such as the imminent threat of a tiger lurking nearby or a freezing chill in the air, and instinctively reacted to the information, perhaps by running in the other direction, or building a fire. We still rely on the instinctual part of our brains every day, and its input can be vital to our survival. However, as civilizations formed and grew increasingly more complicated, it was necessary for our brains to also evolve. The insightful part of our brains (the PFC in particular) has vastly expanded in size and scope, and plays a vital role in evaluating the complex social and cultural situations that have become part of our modern world.

The Hazards of a Primitive Brain in a Modern-Day World

There's inherent danger in your instinctual brain taking over. Once your amygdala and your thalamus (in your limbic system) pick up sensory information (sight, sound, smells), they decide whether it is "good" or "bad" in less than 1/10th of a second. This instinctual reaction comes first; then the message is conveyed to your insightful cerebral cortex that it's been handled or that it's a situation that requires further evaluation (because your instinctual brain cannot determine what a particular stimulus means to your safety and survival). Those initial stimulus evaluations are rooted in, and colored by, millions of years of evolution and can be way off base in our present-day situations. Therefore, you don't want your instinctual, reflexive brain making all the decisions, particularly when those decisions relate to the complexities of wealth creation.

However, it is easy for your more primal, instinctual brain to take control over your more highly developed, reflective brain, causing you to make hasty decisions based on heightened emotions—as we had to do for millions of years—rather than making decisions based on knowledge, logic, and integrated evaluation, as has become necessary only much more recently. Thus, it's up to you to recognize this danger so that you can take control and use your insightful (reflective) brain, not your instinctual one, when making financial decisions.

How This Relates to Getting Rich

When it comes to generating wealth, you are—almost always—well advised to rely on your insightful brain, not your instinctual brain. The challenge arises when emotional triggers in your environment (the stock market plummets; a significant reversal in your business occurs; you see the results of a poor investment decision; your friends continually bemoan the current state of the economy) or internal stimulation (feeling frightened when your boss comes storming into your office, triggering a resurgence of your negative failure script) cause your reflexive, instinctual brain to take over.

This becomes particularly dangerous when serious mental reflection and control are needed, as in the following scenarios:

- Deciding whether to fight back when your boss insults you.
- Committing to an extra line of credit to keep your business afloat.
- Riding the ups and downs of the stock market without jumping in and out at the wrong time.
- Resisting the temptation of blowing your budget to pay for a big-ticket item, just because you are feeling down and need immediate gratification to perk you up.

In these situations, as in many others related to managing your finances, circumventing your more highly developed, insightful brain can lead to ill-conceived decisions that can cost you dearly. So, with that understanding, let's explore the ways you can consciously call upon your more evolved, reflective brain to make wealth-creating financial decisions.

TAKE CHARGE OF YOUR BRAIN

Decision-making creates a state of imbalance in your brain functioning and because your brain likes closure, it will naturally seek the most efficient way (with the least emotional or cognitive cost) to return to a state of equilibrium.

On the Flip Side

Your instinctual, reflexive brain isn't always driven by fear or other negative emotions. Sometimes it's quite the opposite. It can also be stimulated by razzle dazzle, sending your more insightful brain messages that this is a great opportunity, and the strength of those messages may be so powerful it will make you oblivious to contradictory evidence, even when the evidence is quite potent or is easily perceived by others as highly risky. In those situations, it's also wise to slow down and consciously engage your insightful brain to more carefully evaluate the situation.

Also, if your brain becomes too saturated with stress chemicals to invest the required energy for thoughtful, reflective decision-making, it will revert to the easier, instinctive responses. When you aren't under undue pressure, personally or financially, and are not under time restraints, your insightful, reflective brain is more likely to make itself heard. However, when your stress barometer starts to rise and your insightful brain isn't coming up with answers fast enough, your brain's "quick-and-easy" predilection may kick the task back to your instinctual brain, which will rely on sensory or emotional cues, rather than nuance or subjectivity.

That's why when you need to assimilate and understand the most salient points, you should never rush yourself, or allow anyone else to rush you. If you are not someone who has invested time in the world of financial education, it is natural to have a more deliberate learning curve and require time for further explanations and education, as well as time to process the information in your unique learning style. When it comes to money, you want your insightful PFC to marshal its forces. Stress-reducing activities—meditation, mindfulness, breathing exercises, positive visualization, mental rehearsal, and thought control, as we discuss throughout the book—will help your brain strengthen reflective processing. A more extensive listing of actionable ideas can be found in Appendix A: Specific Things You Can Do to Train Your Brain to Get Rich.

OVERRIDE YOUR BRAIN'S OBSESSION WITH PATTERNS

You've heard the expression "everything happens in threes." Well, there's a reason we so readily believe this, even if there is little objective proof that it holds true. A module in the left hemisphere of your brain is programmed to search for patterns and to see causal relationships, even when none exist.

Because your instinctual, reflexive brain frequently dominates in this task, you often look for patterns without realizing it, and if you see a pattern, your brain tends to accept it as fact. For example, when something entirely new happens for the first time (say, you get an extra five-dollar tip the first time you smile at a customer), your brain wonders if there is causation ("I wonder if that will happen again, if I smile again?"). If you smile again and get the same response, your brain reflexively reacts ("Ah-ha! I was right!"), and jumps to what it thinks is a logical conclusion ("It was the smiling that got me the tip!"), thereby linking the perceived pattern to causality. Thus, instead of an "I wonder" response from your insightful brain, you get an "I know" response from your instinctual brain. So, you begin to expect rather than think.

Why Random Activity Leaves Us Feeling Unsettled

Many studies show that people have a difficult time drawing truly "random" patterns. If we asked you to make random marks along a line, because your brain is so wired to see patterns, you'd have to try really hard to make it "look random" and would end up making some sort of pattern, no matter how hard you resisted. Even if you had succeeded in drawing something truly random, you would probably think it looked like a pattern and would alter it, thus *making* it a pattern! It's practically impossible to complete the task successfully because our brains don't even really know what random looks like.

Recognizing patterns and connecting them to past occurrences helped primal man survive, and those who watched for, noticed, and heeded patterns lived to pass on their genes, which wired the survival skill in their instinctual, reflexive brain—a brain you have inherited.

Unfortunately for us, we look for patterns and connections automatically and pretty much unconsciously. You can't turn it off, but you can learn to recognize when it's occurring, and enlist your insightful brain's evaluative skills to override the compulsion to attach patterns and meaning to randomness.

Minimize Unconscious Conformity Bias

Your brain wants to find patterns, because a predictable life makes it more likely for you to survive and pass on your genes. This is why humans are subject to something that is called "conformity bias," meaning that we interpret information to conform to the patterns our brain has set up, because it is easier and also reaffirms established beliefs. For example, to extend the metaphor above, let's say you smile at the third customer that comes into the restaurant, but receive no tip at all. Instead of thinking "Oh, perhaps I was wrong about smiling being the source of my tip," you are likely to think "Well, that person was just rude! Smiling again to another person will get me a tip!"

Tone Down Emotional Reactions

Once your brain decides that responses are predictable, your brain responds with alarm if the apparent pattern is broken, even if it was never a real pattern. And if you have an emotional reaction, your reflexive brain may take over, creating unnecessary panic and overreaction.

Also, your instinctual or reflexive brain is so astute when it comes to recognizing similarities it will jump to attention when it encounters something different, or something it cannot quickly place into context. When that happens, your instinctive brain can make such a ruckus you stop whatever you are doing and pay attention to whatever it has found so alarming.

Understand that this is the part of your brain that wants to interpret events and data to make sense of the world. It believes that it can and will figure things out, but a constant search for explanations and patterns in random or complex data can lead to poor financial decision-making.

Here's how you can tame your reflexive circuit when you are facing important financial decisions:

- Beware of emotionally charged, excitatory language.
- Don't automatically keep going back to the same investment expecting the same return.
- Set limits on how much you'll invest, no matter how good it sounds.
- Control exposure to fluctuating information (turn off CNBC, don't have a ticker running at the bottom of your screen).
- Create a checklist of standards that must apply to all investments and stick to it.
- Take a hard look at the probabilities.
- Think twice . . . and then three times.

REIN IN TREE-SEARCH PROCESSING

Your brain is only as good as its ability to store memories, link information, and comprehend complexity. Unfortunately, your brain also has a predilection for tree-search processing—endlessly following thought streams to collect all conceivable data—which leads to unnecessary and often crippling indecisiveness.

Basically, when your reflexive brain has received, processed, and linked nuggets of information, the neurons branch off and link strongly together. When new information arrives and is linked to the original information, your reflexive brain adds more branches. The next time you need to process information, your brain feels compelled to search all available branches—right out to each branch's tiniest tip—until it has exhausted its storehouse of knowledge.

It's why some people get lost in the details, "instructing" their brains to search each branch to obtain every ounce of information, which can bog down their brain and hamper their ability to make decisions. It can take time and training to overcome this instinct, to realize which information is pertinent to the situation, and which information is not necessary. Training in mindfulness helps direct attention and energy toward the more relevant bits of knowledge so that your brain will not become lost in information overload.

Limit Distractions

Studies have shown that making decisions while also focused on another brain-related task makes it easier for your reflexive (instinctual) brain to overpower your reflective (insightful) brain. That's why being solely focused on what pertains to a decision is essential when making choices that will have a long-term financial impact. Your brain's CEO needs focus to evaluate the situation and override whatever your reflexive brain may be clamoring for you to do. An unfocused brain is more susceptible to impulsiveness.

EVALUATE RISK CAREFULLY

We have an innate dislike for uncertainty, stemming from the consequences our ancestors suffered when they faced physical, life-threatening challenges. If they migrated to an area where rain was sporadic or too many predators lurked in nearby bushes, they would soon be dealing with the prospect that their food sources could run out, or that they wouldn't have enough water to drink, or that they would be killed. This uncertainty kept their brains on high alert, pumping out chemicals that created a low-level, constant state of fearful anticipation and relying on a hair-trigger response to threats. While surely not idyllic, this hypersensitivity increased survival rates.

In ancient times, those people who fixated on gains over losses may have been happier, but those who fixated on safety, preventing the loss of valuable resources or minimizing the amount of offspring killed by wild animals or disease or famines, stuck around a lot longer, and passed on their risk-adverse genes. Because your brain tends to equate money to resources such as shelter, food, or security, your brain responds to money loss in the same way it would respond to a sudden famine or a collapsed shelter. Thus, when confronted with monetary risks, your instinctual brain will most likely recoil from the very idea.

Why You'll Opt for Stable over Unstable

Dogs, like all animals, possess a keen sensitivity to impending danger. It's why they are so highly attuned to sights, sounds, movement, and smell. When sensory input—or genetic hard-wiring—indicates a potential for danger, both animal and human brains respond instantly. While animals don't have a concept for money or monetary rewards, their brains do react to the availability of food and water. And, if they sense that availability is in question, research has shown that most will opt for a steady source of food and water over a bounteous, if unstable, source. Most humans have the same tendency, opting for a sure thing over a risky thing, even if the risk/reward ratio is reasonably favorable.

Also, financial losses are processed in the same region of your brain that responds to mortal danger, which means emotions run high when financial loss looms. Being too fearful, however, can lead to lost opportunities. Although there is a range of difference in the comfort individuals have in taking risks, the tendency to be risk averse is far more common, and, as it comes into play quite unconsciously, it may be limiting your financial options. When it comes to investing, if you remain too cautious, your bills will be paid but there probably will not be the financial excess that permits your money to make money—the secret to becoming rich.

Why You Occasionally Love to Take Risks

Evolution has naturally designed your brain to pay closer attention to rewards when they come surrounded by risks. Your brain doesn't evaluate potential gains in isolation. It assesses your potential outcomes not just against what did happen but also against what *might* have happened. The chance that you could have lost money makes earning money even sweeter. On the flip side, if you picked four of the five numbers on this week's lottery, your brain may prod you to double up on tickets next week, because you *might* have won—if you'd only had that one last number!

What You Need to Know about Risk

You may not realize how your brain evaluates and analyzes risk. Understanding how your brain sees risks can help you present information to your insightful brain in such a way that it is more likely to realistically assess the risk. Here's what you need to know:

- Your brain reacts very differently to odds expressed as percentages compared to odds expressed as frequencies, mostly because it's hard to visualize a percentage, but also because framing can elicit emotional responses. For instance, if someone tells you new businesses fail at a ratio of 6:1, it sounds less risky than if someone tells you there's only a 16 percent chance you'll succeed. Even more telling, if they quote an 84 percent chance that you'll fail, you'll likely give up the idea entirely.

- The less money you have, the more risk you're willing to take. Research has shown that our insula becomes more heavily activated (giving us a feeling of disgust and aversion) with higher and higher stakes. When you have less, you have less to lose.
- Your brain doesn't like to lose. Your insula often deals with absolutes rather than percentages. For instance, the feeling of losing $10,000 will always be worse than the feeling of losing $1,000—no matter what percentage of your income or profits those numbers represent.

Why Suppressing Fear Helps You Make Better Decisions

Your body has an arsenal of chemicals—good guys and bad guys, if you will. When you feel anger, and especially panicky fear, your instinctual, limbic system unleashes cortisol, a stress hormone that sends a bottom-up alert through your regulatory systems to assess threat and options, initiating your fight-or-flight response and tamping down your ability to think rationally, making any sort of calm, logical decision virtually impossible. On the flip side, optimism, hope, and confidence unleash serotonin, which promotes calm and allows your brain to take the time to think things through. Choose your weapons with careful thought!

Risk Management

It's up to you to consciously push past instinctual fear and call upon your evaluative, insightful PFC to more thoroughly assess risk, removing as much emotion as possible from the decision. Sometimes risks are dangerous, but your instinctual brain may be sounding an alarm based on unsubstantiated fears; it's up to you to maximize your brain's evaluative skills when making the final decision.

DON'T LET FEAR RUN THE SHOW

Fear creates a visceral experience, and it's contagious, so potent it gives the common cold a run for its money. Reading about bad news—a violent crime, war, economic, environmental, or medical disasters—is enough to cause the person reading it to more than double their estimates of the likelihood of risks entirely unrelated to the bad news they just read. For instance, reading about a recent bad earthquake across the globe can cause you to suddenly worry about your health, marriage, or children. Bad news makes you hypersensitive to anything that even reminds you of risk, even if the risk is nonsensical or remote. In a similar vein, researchers have even found when national soccer teams lose a big match, the losing country's stock market suffers a downward dip the next day.

Why Decisions Should Sometimes Wait

Studies have shown that roughly 50 percent of people can recognize when they have been disturbed by a bit of negative news, but only 3 percent admit that being upset may influence how they react to other risks. Evidence proves quite the contrary—that we are definitely affected by bad news. That means our brains trick us into thinking we've got it all under control. If you've just experienced bad news, hold off on important decisions until your emotions have time to quiet and your brain isn't coping with stress chemicals.

What Fear Does to Your Brain

When your primitive brain feels afraid, that fear takes precedence, virtually eliminating your brain's ability to perform critical thinking functions. Your amygdala, which is genetically wired to put fear at the top of any to-do list, ignores other sensory input until you have resolved the fearful situation. This is particularly problematical when your fear is occurring at an unconscious level, and you aren't even aware that your PFC has stopped functioning. It can often feel like paralysis brought on by low-level anxiety, and those who suffer from ADD are particularly susceptible, which is why they have trouble paying attention.

Whether or not you are aware that you're feeling fearful, or whether or not there's an actual reason for feeling so afraid, your amygdala sends out distress signals to your PFC, which shuts down critical thinking. You lose your ability to focus on even simple tasks. Instead, your brain is searching for the cause of the fear and for anything else in your environment that feels threatening. In other words, your primitive brain is on high alert, and your conscious, thinking brain is on hold.

How to Quiet Your Amygdala

To overcome this tendency, it's important to quiet your amygdala's predilection for focusing on fear. There are a number of tactics you can use, such as visualization, meditation, mental rehearsal, relabeling, and soothing, loving-kindness mantras. Learning to recognize your fear (or situations that might create fear, even unconscious fear) offers you the opportunity to tamp down an overactive amygdala. By anticipating fearful situations and imagining (whether through visualization, meditation, or mental rehearsal) successful outcomes, you lay the neural groundwork, a neural path, if you will, that your brain can follow when panic strikes.

Basically, it works like this:

- Visualization creates neuronal pathways that counteract a more instinctual neuronal rut, helping future events go more smoothly.
- Meditation (see Chapter 9) increases your ability to recognize fears as they arise, be more aware of your thoughts and emotions and how to keep them under control. It also increases oxytocin, which bolsters trust.
- Mental rehearsal (see Chapter 8) helps you feel prepared for any situation, increases confidence, and lays a neuronal pathway for success.
- Relabeling a situation can affect your emotional response. If you are faced with a "problem," you may feel overwhelmed, but if you call the same situation a "challenge," your competitive nature will rise to the occasion.
- Loving-kindness or self-compassionate meditation creates positive emotions that will calm your amygdala in stressful situations.

Meanwhile, Act As If You're Not Afraid

Highly successful people tend to circumvent fear and focus on using their brains to come up with innovative solutions. They table their fear and invest in their intellectual and resourceful abilities to generate whatever ideas, resources, or money will be required to forge ahead. They don't become mired down in pessimistic outlooks. Where some see insurmountable problems, they see opportunity.

You can rewire your brain to stop reacting out of fear. Taking positive action to avoid fear-based reactivity will help you build a neural network focused on profit (rather than loss). Fear triggers an instinctual response from your reflexive brain. To offset this initial reaction, you need to analyze the basis for the fear. With the help of your insightful, reflective resources you can break your habitual fear-based patterns, and make decisions, whenever possible, based on cold, hard facts.

Understand Your Working Memory's Limitations

Your working memory is concerned with what's happening right now—the four or so facts that you can hold in your head at any given time. It can be so attuned to what's occurring—and seeking immediate solutions or additional stimulation, or getting tied up in emotional backlash—that your brain never really has time to kick into gear and let you hold on to a rational thought. Here's how your memory works, along with its limitations:

- Your short-term memory is what's happened in the last couple of minutes (which you're still deciding if you need to remember).
- Your long-term memory is anything you've decided to retain over five minutes or so and assigned your brain to file and link to similar information.
- Your working memory—the few facts that you're holding on to from moment to moment—will shut down until you have dealt with whatever fearful emotions are happening in the moment, and thus cannot register other forms of information, like context or calming cues.
- When your basal ganglia are busy responding to fear and panic and have flooded your brain tissue with cortisol, your insightful brain isn't free to seek creative ideas and solutions.

By understanding its limitations, you can afford your working memory the time and space it needs to support you in various situations—and improve your ability to focus on the facts you need to remember.

BEWARE OF FALLING INTO NEURONAL RUTS

As we've described, your brain can become set in its ways and respond rigidly to new situations. Fear can amplify and compound this problem by releasing cortisol, which can squash ideas before they are given fair consideration. When fear turns into full-blown panic, any desire for innovative solutions falls sway to an onrush of emotions. Even worse: Your basal ganglia can also "remember" past episodes of panic and become more reactive to cortisol and other stress hormones after each panic episode, which means it will take less cortisol (or fear) on each subsequent occasion for you to still launch into fight-or-flight mode. This makes it very hard for you to take risks, even when they are relatively safe risks. Also, your creativity bites the dust—and this can become your habitual pattern, which your brain accepts and reinforces.

The Solution

If you find yourself in a rut of fear, put yourself in new, interesting, or even slightly risky situations so you can learn to overcome your fears and retrain your working memory to focus on the facts of the situation, rather than your emotional response to them. If you still fall sway to fear, adopt calming methods, such as deep breathing, labeling your fears, challenging assumptions, and waiting until you are able to see the situation in a new light.

With concentrated attention and practice, your brain will smooth over those reactive ruts and you will find it easier to put fear in perspective and engage your insightful PFC when it's needed for evaluation and nuanced thinking.

TEACH YOUR BRAIN TO AVOID THE SAME MISTAKES

Because your brain seeks predictable patterns, you may find yourself making the same financial mistakes over and over again, thwarting your efforts to get rich. Your brain actually prefers predictability and patterns—even when they result in negative consequences!

Do What the Frugal People Do

Several behavioral studies have found that making a list, or engaging in some form of preshopping preparation, prevents overspending. Strategizing, researchers say, can reduce what you spend by as much as 30 percent, and it can be as simple as adopting similar behavior of those who, shall we say, pinch their pennies. Before buying, the more frugal among us would likely weigh their options by factoring in the opportunity cost of the money they're about to spend ("If I buy this $100 gadget today, I won't be able to spend $100 impressing my girlfriend on our next date, or, more important, I won't have an extra $100 to put into an investment account so my money will be working for me instead of the retailer.") This "either-or" strategy is an example of creating a more productive balance between your brain's reflective and reflexive processing.

To combat this tendency, make your brain very aware of these types of mistakes. Take time every so often to make a list of your financial mistakes. Ask yourself: "What are the negative money-related habits I fell into that had absolutely no value, and in fact were detrimental to my overall finances?" Some of these might include:

- Not paying attention
- Making hasty decisions
- Obsessively researching
- Letting fear guide choices
- Ignoring signs that action is needed

- Stressing out instead of confronting problems
- Succumbing to brain chatter instead of rational thought

Once you have your list, make a conscious decision and an action plan to learn from those mistakes. You will grow as a money manager and investor—and your brain will even help you to focus on solutions and search for ideas that will support your quest.

CHOOSE YOUR FOCUS

What you focus on becomes what your brain focuses on. You can train your brain to think creatively, expand, and grow, or you can train it to be focused on fear and avoiding risk, which is likely to lead to lost opportunities and stagnation. It all depends on what you let into your brain—those four things you are thinking of each moment—and how you choose to respond to each. You have the ability to either dumb down your brain or challenge your brain, and your brain will cooperate, by falling into the same neuronal ruts and automatically reinforcing your negative views, or by opening up new neuronal pathways to meet the challenges you ask it to address.

Take the Long View

Economists have identified a phenomenon they call the behavior gap, which can impair your financial returns on investments. Studies have shown that the real-life return of the average investor is dramatically lower than the return of the average mutual fund. It happens because individual investors lack the objective discipline of the professional and tend to let fear and other emotions overrule their thinking. That means they may sell stock when it cycles down, thereby missing out on long-term gains when it cycles back up; and they have a greater tendency to chase returns by constantly searching for hot stocks. They are using their reflexive thinking rather than reflective; whereas mutual fund managers are trained to keep their focus on seeking long-term gain and will not let their reflexive responses take over. To make sure your brain stays focused on the long view and isn't so susceptible to chasing returns, try the following strategies:

- Create a personal investment strategy that incorporates both short-term and long-term goals.
- Base your financial decisions on what is likely to happen in the long-term—the next decade, or several decades, depending on how much time you have.
- Pick an asset allocation strategy that fits your investment statement (strategy) and put money into the appropriate funds.
- Keep your fees low by keeping your trading low.
- Rebalance your account each year.

It may sound simple, but it takes discipline to stick to your plan and not get distracted by scary downturns, hot trends, and promises of big returns.

WATCH ADDICTIVE TENDENCIES

Experiencing a huge gain can feel so good that your brain immediately (and soon compulsively) seeks opportunities to recreate the experience. The lure of the thrill—and the dopamine and serotonin brain baths that accompany it—can lead to an unhealthy focus on chasing big returns, or ever-new ways to make big money, or garner even more prestige. You can literally become so driven by your quest for wealth that the quest itself (rather than the reward) becomes addictive; and, if not addressed and resolved, eventually puts your total financial security at risk. When you're raking in big money, the effect on your brain is the same as if you were taking hard drugs.

Why Gambling Is So Addictive

Money is a reward, and thus reactions to it are rapidly processed in your reflexive brain, which is highly responsive to the amount of reward at stake and much less sensitive to changes in the probability of receiving the reward. A good example of this is in gambling, especially with slot machines. Let's say that every time you spin the slot machine, there's a 1 in 1,000 chance of getting the jackpot. If you spin it again, you still have a 1 in 1,000 chance, but your brain tends to think that the probability is going to be higher, that every miss is bringing you closer to a win. In fact, the probability remains static: It's always 1 in 1,000.

The high associated with receiving a random reward, coupled with the continual anticipation of receiving an additional reward keeps gamblers in a state of high excitement. That leads directly to decreased reflective judgment. And it is why the casino owners, not the players, have smiles on their faces.

LEARN TO RECOGNIZE MANIPULATIVE STRATEGIES

Your brain reacts when it hears words that are designed to incite it to act. Stock market analysts use action verbs like "climbing" or descriptions like "going through the roof" to create an emotional response in listeners. They employ sophisticated marketing experts to give them just the right kinds of messaging to send.

Inflammatory words create emotional responses, invoking your instinctual brain's attention, which neutral words don't. Your brain responds to neutral words more slowly and more reflectively, giving you a chance to use your brain's evaluative skills. If they're appealing to your emotions, it may be because they don't want you to use your insightful brain to evaluate the offer. Remaining on the alert for emotional context will help you call upon your PFC for its evaluative skills, even in the heat of the moment.

Turn Off the TV

Your instinctual, reflexive brain is far more likely to overpower your insightful, reflective brain when stock prices are ratcheting up or plummeting down—and you're listening to minute-by-minute analysis from hyperactive pundits who are using inflammatory language or graphics. In 1999 and 2000, dot.com investors lost at least $30 billion by rushing to buy technology-sector mutual funds that pundits were loudly proclaiming to be "hot, hot, hot." Financial shows can be informative, but they also want higher ratings and will amp up the hype to keep you riveted. Turn off the TV, or radio, or Internet, and quietly mull over decisions before pressing the buy or sell button.

AVOID HERD MENTALITY

Humans are susceptible to a herd mentality, picking up verbal or visual cues from those around them. In other words, you tend to do what everyone else is doing, whether or not you have paused to evaluate the true situation or make a thoughtful decision. While we may not live in herds anymore, the behavior is still very much alive in us. So much so that commissioned brokers anxious to stir up business will use the phrase: "The trend is your friend." This phenomenon was clearly evidenced in the Madoff debacle. Investors were so caught up with the fact that friends, colleagues, and other high-profile names were involved in the Madoff investment schemes that they did very little due diligence, and of course the results proved disastrous. If you want to make more money than most people, succumbing to herd mentality is not going to get you there.

In more recent history, millions of people suffered the real estate bubble when they believed that they, too, could flip a house in days and make a killing. The same economic crisis brought down huge investment firms, who themselves had bought into the same mentality. Every hot streak reaches a saturation point, and every downswing can be exaggerated. It's important to step back from the emotional rush and call upon your insightful brain to calmly and rationally evaluate the situation.

WHAT IT ALL MEANS

You don't have to remember every factoid we present in this book, but you will be far more financially successful if you understand how your brain works and fully appreciate the differences between your reflexive and reflective brains and how they can unduly affect your financial decisions. You want both parts of your brain to work together, balancing feeling with thinking, to evaluate options and make intelligent, thoughtful decisions. Always remember that your reflexive brain will initially respond to flashy or emotional messages, and that it will always be easier to follow its nose than to engage your reflective or analytical brain.

However, as we'll discuss in the next chapter, you can take specific actions to tame your reflexive brain and bolster the ability of your reflective brain to take charge. Turn the page, and we'll get to work!

CHAPTER 8
WORK HARD TO GET RICH

Principle: Your brain has the ability to grow in accordance with your needs, or as a result of what you do to stimulate it.

Of the many facts we've told you about your brain, the one we intend to address in this chapter is the laziness of your brain. If left to its own devices, it tends to seek the easy solution. And wouldn't you know it? The easy solution is often the one your quick-responding instinctual brain provides. That means your conclusions can be driven by emotions, rather than based on all of the pertinent information in any situation. In the last chapter, we talked about how to make more rational, logical decisions—by learning to quiet your gut-check responses based on fear, risk aversion, or panic and turning on your reflective, thinking brain to make choices based on logic, analytical thinking, and facts.

In this chapter, we're going to go a step further and explain how you can engage your PFC more often, thereby training your insightful brain to use all of its resources to think longer and harder. That will help you make sound financial decisions or craft ingenious career strategies. This means you have to build your insightful brain's neuronal pathways, and focus on using it more than relying on your instinctual brain to solve problems for you.

DON'T OVERLOAD YOUR BRAIN

These days, everyone's brain is being seriously taxed, but some overwhelm their brains more than others. To see how you're doing, take the following quiz.

The *Is My Brain on Overload?* Quiz

1. **When it comes to multitasking, I:**
    A. juggle about five things at once.
    B. do pretty well if it's not more than three things at once.
    C. know I'm over my limit if I'm trying to do two things at once.
    D. never multitask when I'm working on something important.

2. **I check my incoming e-mails:**
    A. the second they come in.
    B. every hour on the hour.
    C. about five times a day.
    D. twice a day.

3. **When I get an e-mail that requires a detailed response, I:**
    A. shoot them a response that I'm overwhelmed and they'll have to wait.
    B. stop whatever I'm doing and answer, sans specifics.
    C. place a check mark by it and try to remember to come back to it later, when I have what I need to answer it.
    D. place it in my "immediate response needed" file and jot down what I need to collect to answer it.

4. **When my boss wants to know why my department is so far behind, I:**
   A. get angry and defensive.
   B. panic and make up excuses, whether they're true or not.
   C. tell her that we have several issues that need to be addressed and request a meeting the next day, after I've had time to collect my thoughts.
   D. tell her I'll send her a memo and promptly make up a list of the problems, along with ideas to resolve them.

5. **When I have to learn something new, I:**
   A. make a lot of noise about how unhappy I am about this.
   B. postpone it as long as possible.
   C. do my best to clear enough brain space.
   D. see it as a marvelous challenge.

6. **When I have to evaluate a product's viability, I:**
   A. don't have a clue where to begin.
   B. ask my superior what I'm supposed to say.
   C. research online for the next three days, compiling as much information as possible, even if it is only remotely related to the product.
   D. research the success of similar products and extrapolate ideas to come up with my own conclusion.

Answer Key

If you checked mostly As, you aren't giving your brain an opportunity to fire up—let alone get you through your day. You are a victim of information overload and your emotional responses and inefficiency can be vastly improved, if you give your brain a chance to work its magic.

If you checked mostly Bs, you have too much going on simultaneously and your poor brain is feeling the pressure. You—and your brain—will function at a much higher level when you get your workload under control and use your brain to its best advantage.

If you checked mostly Cs, even if you're coping fairly well and not feeling overwhelmed, you have too much on your plate. Your brain needs you to be its watchdog, making sure it's being given the time and space it needs to make you both successful.

If you checked mostly Ds, you have a handle on priorities and are fairly good at managing tasks. However, with a little more attention to your brain, you'll discover a font of creativity and innovation that will power you to the next level.

ENGAGING YOUR REFLECTIVE (INSIGHTFUL) BRAIN

One quick way to kick your insightful brain into gear is to search harder for evidence that something is not true rather than search for evidence that it is true. Your reflexive (instinctual) brain doesn't like uncertainty and will quickly reframe problems into terms it can understand and answer with ease, usually into simple, easy-to-categorize "truths" that are probably not true under real-world circumstances. To make smart financial decisions, you want to use your reflective brain to counteract emotional rushes to judgment incited by oversimplified instinctual responses. If you focus on proving something is not true, or at the very least thinking of ways that it might not be true, your insightful PFC has to snap to attention and bring all of its evaluative skills to the table.

For example: If an investment counselor is pitching a certain stock, and you ask if it will keep going up over a period of time, he may pull out a chart displaying an upward trajectory over the last six months. The colorful and dramatic graphics alone may be enough for your reflexive brain to eagerly issue a "buy" command. However, all the chart *really* shows is that the stock went up over the last six months, not that it will do so in the next six months.

To do its fair share, your reflective brain would want a lot more factual information, such as how the stock performed over a longer period of time, or the percentage of increase over the past year, or two years, or what the entire market has done during that same period of time. However, even with all that information, your original question about whether the stock will *keep* rising will not be answered.

Your reflexive brain might be dazzled, but given time your insightful, reflective brain is far more likely to realize that no one can truly answer your original question, which is whether the stock will keep rising. No one can know the answer to that, since none of us can see into the future. However, if you give your insightful brain a chance, you can dig deeper and evaluate the stock's realistic potential to continue posting gains. To make this evaluation, you will need more information than advertisements and colorful graphics that contain little information and are only designed to incite your more emotional, reflexive brain to do their bidding. This why when dealing in the world of finance, you should challenge your reflective brain with additional financial education so that you will know what you don't know and will know what information you need to add to your decision-making repertoire.

HOW TO GET YOUR PFC IN THE GAME

What you need to make good decisions in these "Act Now!" situations is to get your insightful PFC in the game. One quick way to call in your more highly evolved, thinking brain is to ask a lot of follow-up questions, even if they seem dumb. If the financial counselor responds with terminology you don't understand, stop and ask the counselor to explain the concept in simpler terms. Your brain is on a learning curve and you need to be sure it's treated respectfully.

Until you can tell the counselor what financial terms mean, you're still learning. Remember the old adage that there are no dumb questions? That's especially true when it comes to learning investments and finance. And don't think that only someone good in math can learn it; the poet can learn it as well as the mathematician can.

Before going into any meeting that will affect your finances, think of at least three questions to ask the person you'll be speaking with, whether it's a mutual fund manager, a job interviewer, or a prospective client. If you're meeting with a fund manager, ask for concrete proof of claims and assertions, for more details, for comparisons to other similar stocks, for how the stock market is performing in general, and how certain business trends are likely to affect it. Come prepared as if you were going to a job interview, and realize that you can't take anything at face or immediate value.

There are, of course, many other ways to engage your insightful PFC in decision-making situations. Some of these include the following.

Quiet Your Emotions

Instead of ignoring your emotions, take note of them, and then find some way to quiet them while your brain processes information. This could be by taking deep breaths, or simply giving them a nod to let them know you are aware they are riled up and you will address their concerns. If your emotions are quaking with desire, treat them as you would a small child begging for a treat—distract them until you can decide if it's a healthy choice. Then, follow through at a later time, listening to the fear and addressing it, as we discussed in Chapter 5.

Distance Your Emotions

Pretend you are making the decision for someone else, like your best friend or your child. This sense of "responsibility" for someone else's well-being will likely wake up your reflective brain and call it to attention.

Think Harder

Avoid "satisficing" (combining satisfy with suffice). Do not just accept the first alternative that seems like it might work. Remember that your brain is looking for the best way to save its energy and will be prone to accept the quickest way to solve the problem or answer the question. Thus, it will present you with a solution that meets minimal criteria for adequacy, rather than doing the work required to identify an optimal solution. If you don't intentionally and fully engage your reflective brain, you can end up with inertia in decision-making, and your brain may even fall back on fear. Thoroughly explore all options—don't just think until you come up with the first "reasonable" solution. Keep thinking after that. Record your ideas on a list so that your brain doesn't just keep recycling them. In many cases, the best solution comes in at number twenty or fifty—or even ninety-nine!—on your list.

Be Savvy

Look beneath fancy packaging. Investment firms use advertising, often showing beautiful people in lavish and attractive settings to imply that you, too, can be rich and beautiful, living a lavish lifestyle—*if* you invest with them. Always look beneath the fancy packaging to see the firm's true performance levels and to evaluate the way they do business, not the way they attract new customers.

Stall for Time

Ask for a time-out. Make it a rule not to make hasty decisions. You can even tell people if they press you for a decision: "I have a policy of considering financial decisions for twenty-four hours before making them." If nothing else, give your brain a good ten minutes to absorb information; this gives your insightful PFC time to kick in. Spend the time deep breathing and calling upon your more rational, reflective brain to engage.

Gather More Information

You absolutely want to gather as much relevant information as you can. The more relevant information you feed your brain, the better it can respond with informed, evaluative assessments. However, avoid analysis paralysis by giving yourself a reasonable deadline to make a decision—a day, a week, a month—depending on how much information you need to make the decision (buying a toaster requires less time than buying a house). See the section later in this chapter called "Make It Easier for Your Brain to Think."

Get a Second Opinion

Two brains are always better than one, particularly if the second person won't be affected by your decision and/or is someone who tends to counterbalance your decisions and will help you ask the right questions. Every good brain can use a skeptic, someone who plays devil's advocate and makes your brain think hard before it commits to something.

Walk It Off

Do something physical. Use your body to distance yourself from an intensely mental conversation. Do something that calms your emotions and grounds you in your body. It gives your brain a respite, increases oxygen and blood flow to your brain, and brings you back to the task refreshed, renewed, and ready to focus.

Sleep on It

If possible, revert to the advice your grandmother probably gave you and "sleep on it." We'll have more in Chapter 12 about how essential sleep can be to your brain and why it really is sound advice to sleep on decisions, particularly major financial decisions. For now, just know that asking your brain to solve a problem before you fall asleep can produce excellent results.

Questions You Need to Ask Yourself

If you are interested in investing in a company (or going to work for a company), a good way to engage your reflective brain is to answer the following questions:

- Do I understand this type of business and its particular challenges and opportunities?
- Would I want to own this type of business?
- How does it measure up to other companies in its field?
- How strong are its competitors?
- What are its strengths . . . and its weaknesses?
- Does it have opportunities for growth and expansion?
- Are there negative business trends likely to affect this company?
- Have I read and understood its financial statements, including what isn't directly stated?
- Are its goals and values in alignment with mine?
- How much do I know about the CEO or financial manager?

In taking time to ponder these questions and sort out your knowledge versus your emotions, you are helping your brain's CEO gather the information it needs to process and understand what's being considered.

When It's Safe to Listen to Your Feelings

The goal isn't to be purely rational about investments or career decisions, as your intuition and feelings are also important in guiding decisions. You want to listen to your emotions and trust your instincts, particularly if they have served you well in the past, but you don't want to let them drive the decision.

Your brain can certainly process any information you feed it, integrate that knowledge, link to relational memories, and offer up a perfectly rational decision, but your brain can also flip to the other extreme and become overly excited by language designed to heighten your emotional investment, or become immobilized by fear or doubt or anger, emotions raging so hotly through your amygdala that any decision you make (if you can even make one) isn't likely to be your best option.

The goal is to achieve a healthy balance between making decisions based on rational knowledge and those based on emotions.

Your Brain and Decisions

To improve decision making, you can improve the functions of your brain that are related to that task. So, for example, since being able to focus helps you make decisions—because you need to concentrate on the decision and on the facts needed to make the decision—any effort you make to improve your focus, even if you're just focusing on emptying the dishwasher or reading a book, will eventually improve your decision-making skills. Your brain's skills are transferrable! So what follows are the major brain functions related to decision making. Consider how you can build them up.

- **The ability to focus:** How well you can drown out distractions and focus on the task at hand affects your ability to absorb information.
- **The ability to control your thoughts:** How well you can slow down, speed up, or contain the flow of information running through your brain can all affect how well you think.
- **The ability to process new information:** How well you comprehend new information can affect your decisions.
- **The ability to integrate information:** How you connect new information to what you already know affects the amount of information available to your thinking process.

- **Short-term memory:** Your ability to retain new information could affect your decision-making processes, particularly if you have to absorb a lot of information and make decisions quickly.
- **Long-term memory:** How you think about money and make decisions can be vastly influenced by painful or happy memories and how much emotional charge is connected to them.
- **The ability to develop new skills:** Keeping your brain firing on all pistons keeps it supple and makes it easier to learn new skills.

We have been, and will continue, offering ways for you to improve how well your brain functions, but it's up to you to deliver the muscle, to put the ideas and suggestions into practice and work much harder to fully engage, challenge, teach, train, and nourish your brain. As with all things, those who work hardest will receive the best results.

WHY MULTITASKING IS MULTITAXING

In today's world, multitasking has become *de rigeur*. We're all trying to juggle as many things at once as we can, because that is now expected of us. Unfortunately, your brain is designed to focus attention on the task it deems most important, usually the one that it thinks is the most closely related to survival. It prioritizes getting away from saber-toothed tigers over brushing your teeth. Makes sense, right? But somewhere along the line, instead of doing one task and then another, humans started trying to do more than one thing at a time, then two things, and then three things, and more. Nowadays we often try to do ten things at a time—with disastrous results (for example, see any study on talking on the cell phone while driving).

The truth is that your brain simply *cannot* focus on more than one task at a time. When you ask it to do so, it doesn't. It switches off between tasks. So, when you're talking on the phone while driving, you may think you're paying attention to both, but you're not. Your brain may be attending to the driving, but then when the person you're talking to says something that needs an answer, your brain switches its attention back to the conversation and ignores the driving completely. Additionally, there's a lag time as the brain switches between each task.

The more tasks you add, the less efficient your brain is, and the less likely it is to focus on the most important task (which explains why people talking on cell phones get into car crashes). Multitasking also ramps up the energy demands on your brain, leaving you feeling depleted afterwards. This is why it's best to eliminate as many distractions as possible whenever you have a task that requires your full attention. It's also why you shouldn't make financial decisions when you're in the middle of eight other things. You're likely to pick the wrong answer!

WHY TOO MUCH INFORMATION CAN LEAD TO BRAIN-FREEZE

Given the glut of information we are all subjected to each day, it's little surprise that scientists are now researching what happens when you have too much information—what is popularly called "analysis paralysis." Feeling like you have too much information to attend to has become such a prevalent condition, the Oxford English Dictionary added an entry for "information fatigue" in 2009. It's not a new phenomenon, but what is new is our realization that information overload doesn't just leave people feeling frustrated and emotionally charged, it actually causes cognitive impairment. Recent research in the science of decision making has shown that too much information can lead to people making objectively poorer choices, and to choices they later regret.

The research has shown that an unconscious system guides many of our decisions, and that it can be sidelined by too much information. It also shows that the incubation of ideas needed for true creativity (incubation that ideally occurs just below your conscious awareness) becomes increasingly difficult when information just keeps pouring in.

Every bit of information presents a three-pronged choice: whether to reply immediately, whether to factor it into an impending decision, or whether to discard it entirely. Your working memory can only hold about four items of information; after that, information deemed worthy of holding on to has to be shuttled to your short-term and perhaps even your long-term memory, which requires a conscious effort. While still accumulating information, your brain begins to struggle with what it should keep for future reference and what it can discard. Ignoring repetitive input and deciphering what is not going to be useful later ties up your cognitive resources—and the more information keeps pouring in, the harder it gets. Let's get specific about the ramifications of information overload.

It's Affecting Your Decisions

We're all being overexposed to an onrush of information, which means our brains are being asked to respond instantly. Your brain tries to keep up—even if it's making bad choices. If your brain is being bombarded, it tends to favor quick over right. Even in business, many accept the notion that a quick decision is the best decision.

It's Screwing Up Priorities

Your brain is wired to notice and respond to change, which means incoming e-mails or text messages put your decision-making brain to work immediately, because your brain usually will assume that the latest news is the most important news. Behavioral economist George Lowenstein of Carnegie Mellon University calls this the "urgency effect;" paying a lot of attention to the most recent information, and discounting what came earlier. Your brain leans to overvaluing immediacy and quantity of thought more than quality of thought.

It's Smothering Your Brain's True Genius

If you are allowing yourself to be besieged by an influx of information, you are more likely to have trouble making the creative leap required for original thought—or to make wise decisions. Your brain needs time to subconsciously integrate new information with existing information and make novel connections or identify hidden patterns. Being bombarded impinges on your ability to think creatively.

Let This Be a Lesson

In a study, MBA students were asked to choose a (make-believe) stock portfolio. They were divided into two groups, one that was inundated with information from analysts and the financial press, and another that saw only stock-price changes. The latter group reaped more than twice the returns of the info-deluged group, whose analytical capabilities were hijacked by too much information and who wound up buying and selling on every rumor and tip. The more data they received, the harder it became for them to sort it all out.

Just thinking about all the thinking that has to be done to process an onslaught of information feels exhausting. Luckily, you can give your brain the breathing space it needs if you:

- Limit the flow of information. Yes you can turn off your cell phone, your iPad, your computer, and your TV.
- Don't have your computer ding every time an e-mail arrives. Check it twice in the morning and twice in the afternoon (or at most only once an hour) and rank e-mails according

to importance. Create a file for those that need immediate attention; one for those that don't require immediate attention but include crucial information you'll need later; and one for those you can sideline.

- Set priorities, particularly when you have a project that needs your full attention.
- Choose your sources carefully. When you have to gather information from a variety of sources, seek out the most reliable sources and disregard the rest.
- Close off the flow of information when you need to be creative and give your brain time to percolate. Do something that doesn't feed into information overload, like taking a walk.
- Don't go with a methodical, conscious process of pros and cons (or whatever basis you use) when deluged with complex information. Instead, give your unconscious brain a chance to mull it all over.
- Establish the most important criteria for each decision, and focus on those components rather than every piece of information that has come in. Remember that information should not be ranked by when it arrived.

GET YOUR GROOVE ON

You've probably had the experience of being in "the zone" or in "the flow," where time flies by as you focus on a task at hand. It often happens when you've been focused on a task for a long time, concentrating on tackling whatever needs to be solved. This doesn't happen independently of preparation, though. If you're a writer who has experienced flow while writing a chapter, it's likely the result of hours you spent rereading and organizing your notes. If you're a graphic artist, the flow comes after you've been leafing through magazines for hours, searching for inspiration. If you're a CEO, the brilliant strategy comes after you've observed carefully as your staff pitched ideas, assimilated all of their ideas, and then formulated your own.

Whatever you do for a chosen profession, there are times when you've put in the preparation, studied the problem from all angles, searched for additional knowledge and inspiration, and then given your brain the time and space it needs to assimilate and order the information. Suddenly you're there—in your own little groove— the place where all your preparatory work has gelled and your brain is firing on all pistons.

You can call it your groove, your zone, being in the flow, or whatever term most appeals to you. Whatever it takes to get there, it's an ideal state for idea generation and creativity. It's when your brain serves up the final recipe—and it all seems to flow out of your mind and onto the table.

How to Know If You're in the Flow

We've all had a taste of the flow, and hopefully, you know how to get yourself in that zone, where you are so immersed and happy doing something that it all flows very smoothly, leaving you feeling satisfied and inspired. Flow is a marvelous tool for creativity and a marvelous example of perfect focus. So how can you tell when you're in the flow?

- You feel extremely confident about and prepared for the task.
- You find it easy to concentrate and feel "at one" with the task.
- You know exactly what you're intent on achieving.
- You become so deeply engaged that you forget about everything else.
- You feel energized, capable, and happy.
- You lose track of time.

It's important to note that flow requires confidence, particularly in knowing that you are up to the task at hand, and enough stimulation and challenge to keep your brain comfortably reaching out for the next idea. Our brains facilitate flow when they feel challenged, but not overwhelmed. If the task far exceeds your capability, it creates anxiety; and if it's too easy, it creates boredom—and both tend to kill the thrill.

GET INTO THE HABIT OF WORKING HARD

If you want to succeed and acquire wealth, make it a habit to fully engage and challenge your mind. Lazy brains aren't as likely to be primed and ready when you need them most. It is very true that the more you use your brain the sharper it becomes. Each use, each introduction of new information, each dip into complex thinking or creativity strengthens existing synapses, creates new synapses, and even creates new neurons. You have the ability to reshape your brain simply by doing the desired tasks on a regular basis, stretching just a little more each time.

Do What the Rich Do

Rich people tend to spend their spare time either doing something that increases their wealth, or studying ways to increase their wealth. In other words, they are extremely "wealth conscious" (looking for ways to generate more wealth), motivated, focused, and hard working.

It's also a truism that the less you do something, the less importance your brain attaches to it. If you stop exercising the parts of your brain required to perform certain tasks, eventually your brain will let those synapses fade into oblivion. You can recall and reactivate many of them (like how to ride a bicycle), and even learn to use other parts of your brain—if necessary—(as stroke victims often have to do), but it's far easier to strengthen existing connections and build new neuronal pathways to success.

Four Ways to Challenge Your Brain at Work
- Every so often, take on a project that feels extremely challenging or intimidating.
- Brainstorm ideas for doing something in an entirely new way.
- Learn a new aspect of the job you already do. For example, if you write fiction, write a poem.
- Learn something completely foreign to you that will challenge you on multiple levels.

So How Long Does It Take to Form a Habit?

According to a 2009 study from University College London, turning a new behavior into a habit requires sixty-six days on average. Easy goals—like eating breakfast of some sort each day—become habitual quickly; but more complicated or challenging behaviors—like writing down what you spend every week in a journal—take a lot longer, as much as nine months, although two months is considered average.

The secret to forming and maintaining a habit is to be extremely dedicated in the beginning stages, and to stick with it, without fail, for at least three weeks. If you stick that long, you have a better chance that the new behavior will become ingrained and eventually habitual.

A few tips:

- Break down the task into easily achievable bites. Instead of writing down what you spend each week, write it down every day, and then post it to your accounting program or file once a week.
- Give yourself the tools needed to do it. If you're writing down what you spend, put a notebook and pencil in your purse or carry an envelope to collect receipts.

- Practice your new behavior at the same time each day, such as right after dinner.
- Create a checklist that you can use to log your successes. Put it on your refrigerator, computer desk, or other place you see every day without fail.
- Reward yourself, appropriately, once a week for sticking with it.
- If you fall off the wagon, get right back on.

You can think of habits as pathways that form over time. For example, if you ride your bike over a dirt road where you've never before been, the tires on your bike will leave a very thin indentation in the dirt that's easily wiped away. However, if you ride your bike down the same path, in the same way, every day, eventually a groove will form that seems like it's always been there. The same applies to neurons—as you form habits, you lay down tracks of neurons on top of each other, strengthening a pathway until it becomes so engrained as to not require thought. It may take a little while, but give it a try and see; soon you'll be coasting down a neuronal highway towards wealth and success, without even realizing you're doing any work at all!

Mom Was Right: Sit Up Straight

Your brain needs nearly thirty times more blood flowing through it than your other organs, and slouching squishes two arteries that transmit blood from your heart, up your spinal column, to your brain. Slouching or leaning over your desk cuts off the blood supply which can quickly lead to foggy thinking and forgetfulness.

SEE BOREDOM AS A CALL TO NEW ACTION

Boredom arises when you have maxed out, learned as much as you can learn or mastered all the skills required to perform your job. Even if you loved your job in the beginning, eventually your brain becomes quite good at performing the required tasks, even to the point of being able to perform while only half-awake (metaphorically). Your brain simply doesn't like repeating the same thing over and over and over. Without challenge, your brain falls into a rut and goes to sleep on the job. This is not quite the same as habits, but boredom can become a habit if you're not careful!

Boredom also breeds boredom. If you want to keep your neurons firing, find something more challenging to do. Ideally, you will find something that challenges your mental abilities—or at least that keeps you using your brain on a daily basis—but doing anything new is beneficial.

So, if you're feeling bored, don't wait for it pass. Boredom is a clear signal from your brain that it needs new or additional stimulation. It's your brain's bid to get your attention. Look for ways to challenge yourself, take on new responsibilities, or find a new job—or at least a hobby that will challenge your brain. Here are three ways to challenge your brain on a daily basis:

1. Commit to doing whatever you undertake to the best of your abilities. Go the extra mile, look for new ways to do ordinary tasks, add nuance to what you're doing, or spend an hour each day learning something new about your profession.
2. Identify holes in your capabilities and fill them.
3. Continually up the ante, challenging your abilities daily.

TRAIN YOUR BRAIN TO DELIVER A DESIRED OUTCOME

One of the oldest precepts of neuroscience has been that our mental processes (thinking) originate from brain activity: that our brain is in charge when it comes to creating and shaping our mind. However, more recent research has shown that it can also work the other way around: that focused, repetitive mental activity can affect changes in your brain's structure, wiring, and capabilities.

The actions we take can literally expand or contract different regions of the brain, firing up circuits or tamping them down. The more you ask your brain to do, the more cortical space it sets up to handle the new tasks. It responds by forging stronger connections in circuits that underlie the desired behavior or thought and weakening the connections in others. Thus, what you do and what you think, see, or feel is mirrored in the size of your respective brain regions and the connections your brain forms to accommodate your needs.

What does all this mean? It means that what we think, do, and say matters; that it affects who we become on the outside, the inside, and in our brain. Mostly, it means that you can retrain your brain to be more productive, more resilient, and more creative.

MENTAL PRACTICE

Professional athletes of all varieties—from football players to swimmers and basketball players to golfers—now routinely perform concentrated mental rehearsals prior to competitions. One of the earliest athletes to embrace mental rehearsals was boxer Muhammad Ali, who developed a unique set of mental skills designed specifically to heighten his performance in the ring. Before a fight, Ali used multiple self-motivational techniques: affirmation; visualization; mental rehearsal; self-confirmation, including his most famous proclamation "I am the greatest" to psyche himself up.

A stunning boxer with a magnetic personality, Ali famously bragged about how he would "whup" his next opponent, usually by reciting seemingly innocuous rhyming couplets. In the months and weeks leading up to a fight, Ali flaunted these rhymes/mantras to fire up the press and, more importantly, to intimidate his opponent. But there was an ingenious method behind Ali's public posturing: Ali was also creating an exacting mental picture of his desired outcome.

In the weeks leading up to his match with George Foreman (who was seven years younger than Ali and buoyed by 2-to-1 odds in his favor), Ali mentally envisioned *his* desired outcome, and, once again, verbally expressed it in the form of rhymes: "He's [Foreman's] got a hard-push punch but he can't hit," Ali crowed, purposefully punching the air in front of a reporter's nose. "Foreman just pushes people down. He just got slow punches, take a year to get there. You think that's going to bother me? This is going to be the greatest upset in the history of boxing." Many scoffed at Ali's bravado and few thought he could pull it off, but Foreman stayed down for the count in the eigth round.

That's because Ali used an arsenal of intention to become a champion. Not only did he believe his own hype, he spent hour upon hour intensely rehearsing fights in his mind—before stepping one foot in the ring. Particularly as age slowed him down, Ali would mentally envision himself warding off his opponent's jabs, breaking down evasions in minute detail, whatever he thought was necessary to bolster what his muscles could do. By the time he entered the ring, he had repeatedly choreographed the fight in his mind. He entered the ring so mentally prepared that his visions often came to pass.

HOW YOU CAN MENTALLY PREPARE

Psychologist Allan Paivio, professor emeritus of the University of Western Ontario, first identified the brain's tendency to use "dual coding" to process verbal and nonverbal information simultaneously. He found that mentally practicing for a sporting event worked as well as physically practicing for patterns and timing in various activities. Paivio's model has been widely adapted to help athletes with motivation or in learning or improving a certain set of skills.

It's Not the Same as Visualization

Although mental rehearsal is often incorrectly seen as synonymous with visualization, visualization can be more removed, as if you are watching a video that features you, or watching yourself through another pair of eyes. For mental rehearsal to work, you have to create strong mental images of being in yourself in the midst of a challenge, feeling or practicing even the tiniest of components kinesthetically. Mental rehearsal is formulating a mental trial run that focuses intently on winning strategies—and culminates in feeling the thrill of victory.

So How Does It Work?

In a quest to solve a scientific conundrum—whether the brain differentiates between a thought and an action—brain researchers wired a group of skiers to electromyography (EMG) equipment, which measures electrical impulses sent from motor neurons to specific muscles. The researchers recorded skiers' neural activity while they skied down a hill, and while they mentally rehearsed skiing down the same hill. They discovered that the skiers' brains sent the same instructions to their bodies whether the skiers were simply thinking of a particular movement or actually carrying it out. Their thoughts produced the same mental instructions as their actions produced.

Research using an electroencephalogram (EEG), which measures electrical activity in the brain, has also shown a similar result: The electrical activity produced by the brain is identical, whether you're thinking about doing something or actually doing it. The same is true for weight lifters. Researchers found that EEG patterns in their brains when they lifted several hundred pounds were identical to those activated by simply imagining lifting the same weight. Just the thought was enough to produce the neural instructions to carry out the physical act.

So I Can Exercise Without Moving a Muscle?

Apparently, you can. Guang Yue, an exercise psychologist at the Cleveland Clinic Foundation, compared nonathletic people who regularly worked out at a gym with nonathletic people who relied solely on mental rehearsal to conduct virtual workouts. Those who regularly worked out at the gym increased their muscle strength by 30 percent; but those didn't go the gym also increased their muscle power, by almost half as much. Subjects between twenty and thirty-five years old merely imagined flexing one of their biceps as hard as they could, five times a week. After ensuring that the participants weren't doing any actual exercise, including tensing their muscles, the researchers discovered an astonishing 13.5 percent increase in muscle size and strength, after just a few weeks, an advantage that remained for three months after the mental training stopped.

Based on this research, scientists proposed that mental rehearsal creates the neural patterns necessary for the real thing. Operating as though the brain were simply another muscle, mental rehearsals train the brain to facilitate the moves more easily during the actual performance.

When an athlete performs, the neurotransmitters that signal to the muscles along a particular pathway are stimulated and the chemicals that have been produced remain there for a short period. Any future stimulation along the same pathways benefits from the residual effects of the earlier connections. We then get better at the rehearsed physical tasks because our electrical signaling has already been forged. Because the brain doesn't distinguish between doing something specific and just thinking about doing it, mental rehearsal lays down the neural pathway just as well as physical practice does. Then, when it comes time to perform, your muscles have the benefit of strengthened synapses and lots of neurotransmitters that are raring to go and put you at your peak—physically or mentally.

The Winning Formula

To be most effective, a mental rehearsal should take place during a state of meditative concentration and hyperawareness and be focused on a highly specific aim or goal. When you imagine this future event, create a mental picture of it as if you were deep in the throes of battle (or victory), engaging all five senses to visualize each aspect that you will have to perform—or react to—in minute detail. Imagining the feel of things in your hands, the tightening of muscles, or even tastes and smells are all very important to laying down a mental foundation. The centerpiece of this mental picture should be the moment you achieve the goal and how grand it feels in your body to have everyone cheering for you. It's important to feel the experience as if it is occurring in your physical body at that very moment.

IMPROVE BRAIN FUNCTION BY LEARNING TO SPEAK A FOREIGN LANGUAGE

After studying bilingual children for years, scientists established that speaking more than one language requires a lot of mental focus and work—and that it pays off in multiple ways. Over time, regularly speaking more than one language appears to create a cognitive reserve, similar to a reserve gas tank in your car. Studies have also found that bilingual children are better at multitasking, and that adults who speak more than one language do a better job prioritizing information in potentially confusing situations.

When you speak two languages you use a brain function known as inhibitory or cognitive control—the ability to stop paying attention to one thing and focus on something else quickly. Fluent speakers of more than one language call upon this skill to silence one language in their minds while communicating in another.

Sorting It Out

To test people's ability to focus while they're simultaneously exposed to extraneous information, scientists use something called the Stroop test. They show subjects the word for a particular color and ask them to identify the color of ink it's printed in. If the word is "blue" and it's printed in blue, it's a cinch. If the word "blue" is printed in red, subjects' brains have to sort out which piece of information—the color of the ink, or the color being spelled out—is the one they need to use to answer the question correctly. In those who only speak one language, switching it up adds 240 milliseconds to their reaction time—a significant delay, in brain reaction terms.

Bilingual people, on the other hand, required only 160 extra milliseconds to sort this out—because they're used to prioritizing information in potentially confusing situations all day.

How It Benefits Your Brain Function

The constant back and forth between two linguistic systems means frequent exercise for your brain's so-called executive control functions in your PFC. This part of your brain is often tasked with focusing your attention, ignoring distractions, holding multiple pieces of information in mind when trying to solve a problem, and then flipping back and forth between them.

Tapping into your cognitive reserve and flexing your brain's cognitive control seems to slow down the onset of dementia. A study published in the journal *Neurology* surveyed 211 patients diagnosed with Alzheimer's and found that those who spoke only one language saw the onset of their first symptoms four to five years earlier than their bilingual peers. While knowing two languages doesn't fight the disease, it does strengthen those parts of the brain that are susceptible to early attacks of dementia, allowing them to withstand the assault much longer. Your brain will still age, just not as fast as in those who don't speak more than one language.

Unfortunately, researchers haven't established whether learning the second language early in life, compared to late in life, makes a significant difference, or whether it's beneficial to learn a second language if you don't speak it fluently on a daily basis. But research has shown that bilingual speaking on a regular basis bolsters your brain's ability to function, even when stressed or damaged.

IMPROVE YOUR FOCUS AND MEMORY

Scientists say we only remember one of out 100 pieces of information that we receive. Our brain has its own "spam filter" in your working and short-term memory to weed out messages it doesn't think are important. However, leaving it up to your brain can be risky because your brain will decide on the basis of what it's been programmed to focus on, or link up, or retain. Unless you consciously reprogram your brain to pay attention to new information, it won't know that it is something you need filed away and/or linked up with existing information.

Alternating Streams

As much as you'd like to believe otherwise, your brain cannot focus sharply on more than one thing at a time. That's why studies proved that people talking on cell phones while driving were 4.3 times more likely to have an accident, and using hands-free devices did not lower the risk. You are never truly doing two things in unison; you are doing two separate things in alternating streams.

Cultivate a Photographic Memory

If you really want to remember something, formulate an extensive mental picture, noticing the smallest details, and recite what you've learned (or noted) later to reinforce the memory. Think back to when you were in school and had to memorize facts; the repetition and the necessity to retain the information was part of your everyday life. If you want to bolster memory retention now, apply the same methods: seeing, hearing, writing down, and repeating the information; linking the new information to existing information; noticing small details; using your senses to strengthen memories; creating rhymes or other creative ways to help you remember what you've just learned, and reinforcing the memory by reciting it later that same day and for a week afterwards.

If you really want to remember something, it's important to focus intently on the subject, and eliminate competing distractions. Even if you think you aren't hearing the music or the TV in the background, your brain is paying attention to whatever is going on around it.

Also, we pay attention to items serially and not in parallel. This means that we tend to focus on one thing, then another, and then another and aren't really able to focus on two things at once (even if we think we can). Further, your brain perks up when searching for event-related items in an array of choices, so "something happening" will immediately strike your interest even if you should be paying attention to something less immediately exciting.

How You Learn

Developing the ability to perform a given task happens in three separate stages.

Learning occurs when you are able to repeat a new behavior in nearly identical situations soon after the original presentation of information has occurred. For example, the teacher tells you that 2 + 2 = 4, and then asks you to tell her what 2 + 2 equals. Ta-da! You have learned something. But that doesn't mean the information does you any good unless you can remember it and apply it to other situations.

Retaining a skill or information occurs when you are able to repeat the new behavior or utilize the information in different kinds of situations and/or after some days have passed. You have retained your skill to add 2 + 2 when your mom asks you the question a week later, while you're in the car on the way the grocery store, and you're able to tell her the answer.

Transferring, or linking the new information to old information or with future learning, occurs when you see a pattern that fits with what you previously learned. Later in the month, your mom is making breakfast. You decide you want two scrambled eggs, and your mom wants two scrambled eggs, so you figure out that your two plus her two equals four eggs and you get four eggs from the refrigerator.

As you can see, these are all different skills, and that's why, for example, you can learn to drive a car under certain conditions (sunny weather) but then have trouble when the conditions change (rain). And it's why you may be able to recite every math fact you learned in fifth grade and still not be able to figure out how much carpet your living room needs.

Your brain does better when you master each step of the learning process before moving to the next level, or to something new.

AND SPEAKING OF LEARNING SOMETHING NEW . . .

It's time to learn the art of mindfulness and mindfulness meditation, two practices that will definitely improve your brain's ability to function. Please, mindfully, turn the page!

CHAPTER 9

MEDITATE TO GET RICH

Principle: Learning to focus your thoughts and moderate your emotions via meditation will help you tamp down an overactive amygdala and strengthen your PFC's ability to focus and function at peak capacity.

It turns out that one of the most effective methods to use your mind to train your brain originated thousands of years ago with the advent of Buddhism. The effects of mindfulness meditation, as practiced by Tibetan monks who still follow the teachings of Buddha (who outlined the principles of mindfulness), are currently being widely researched in the field of neuroscience. Based on these studies, a growing number of neuroscientists believe that the practice of mindfulness meditation in particular may result in positive changes in your brain function.

Buddhist principles define a human being as a constantly changing dynamic stream. Neuroscientists have found scientific proof of neuroplasticity, the ability of our brains to continue to grow and form new synapses, which was once thought impossible in adults. Both Buddhists and neuroscientists now view humans as constantly evolving and capable of expanding and improving upon the way our minds think, and thereby the way our brains work. Learning to harness the idea of mindfulness—that is, living in the present moment—will help you to filter out streams of thought in your brain that have nothing to do with the situation at hand and dedicate your brain space to the "here and now," thereby improving your ability to make smart financial decisions. It also helps you learn to reduce anxiety and be more in tune with other people, both of which will serve you well in the business world. The biggest benefit of mindfulness meditation—or other forms of meditation—however, is that it helps your brain strengthen neural pathways related to achieving your dreams. Meditating will bring amazing reinforcement for your intentions, and strengthen neuronal connections related to that pursuit. So let's backtrack a step and explain more about mindfulness and how it works in general.

ENTER MONEY MINDFULNESS

Mindfulness is the ability to cultivate awareness of the present moment without relying on our usual, somewhat rote perceptions, thoughts, fears, or judgments. It means being in connection with the direct experience of the current moment, being fully present in the here and now—with all of your brain in tune. The practice of mindfulness teaches you how to stay open and learn how to control your own mind, instead of your mind controlling you.

One of its basic tenets is to allow thoughts to come and go, without allowing your mind to latch onto one or the other and lapse into your usual obsessive or reactive tendencies. Mindfulness trains your mind to direct your attention in a wholesome and healthy manner. Whatever is happening in the body (sights, sounds, smells, tastes, sensations) or mind, the task is simply to observe its ever-changing nature.

From birth, our minds learn to interpret internal and external events as good or bad, right or wrong, or fair or unfair. Instead of experiencing events with an open mind, people tend to react to them in a habitual way of perceiving and responding, especially if a new event is similar to an event previously experienced. In other words, how you felt about the original event affects how you think about, experience, and react to similar events—or events that feel similar. Thus it becomes easy to continue to make poor choices and repeat failure patterns. The effect of this cycle on financial decisions can be disastrous and certainly will not contribute to your goal of becoming wealthy.

Mindfulness allows you to become more aware of your habitual thinking processes so you can choose to respond to any situation specifically and individually, and in a way that's most effective for you—in the here and now, leaving problematic money scripts behind.

Mindfulness can be a very effective tool in your quest for wealth. In addition to helping you stay open to the present moment without relying on habitual ways of thinking, feeling, or responding, it helps you notice your thought patterns as they occur, and teaches you how to divert or supplant unproductive thought patterns by focusing on your breath (or your meditation, or a designated object). It helps you learn to refocus on living in the present moment (as opposed to succumbing to rumination or habitual thought patterns).

It's not so much about stopping thought processes as consistently bringing your awareness to what is happening right now. Living mindfully and meditating mindfully can help you defuse negative thought patterns simply by making you aware of them. When you can make decisions without disruptive, biased, or negative thinking, you're more likely to successfully reach your financial goals.

WHY MEDITATE?

Meditation, and particularly mindfulness meditation, supports your quest for wealth by keeping you in top form, mentally, physically, and spiritually. When it comes to making more money, meditation:

- Increases blood flow
- Increases serotonin (the feel-good hormone)

- Decreases cortisol (the feel-stressed hormone)
- Releases creativity
- Increases sense of peace
- Builds awareness
- Bolsters positive thinking
- Creates confidence and wisdom
- Increases insightful thinking
- Improves attention and focus
- Reduces cortical thinning (cortical thinning is related to cognitive problems)
- Increases the building of new synapses

CAPITALIZE ON MEDITATION

Certain ways of thinking (or not thinking) help meditation and mindfulness to do their work.

1. **Cultivate beginner's mind.** This quality of awareness allows you to see things as new and fresh, as if for the first time, with a sense of curiosity.
2. **Surrender judgment.** The goal in mindfulness meditation is to refrain from labeling thoughts, feelings, or sensations as good or bad, right or wrong, fair or unfair, but only to take note of the reality of what is. A nonjudgmental attitude helps you objectively observe your thought processes and emotions.
3. **Surrender striving.** Striving involves being focused on the need to get or be anywhere other than where you are. Mindfulness is all about being very much in the present. Right here, right now.
4. **Maintain equanimity.** Someone with equanimity doesn't get disturbed one way or the other—by positives or negatives. This

quality of awareness allows wisdom, insight, and compassion to rule your actions.

5. **Learn to let go.** Rather than being so focused on outcomes, you can simply let things be as they are with no preconceived ideas of what they should or should not be.

6. **Build self-reliance.** This quality of awareness helps you see for yourself, from your own experience, what is true or untrue. This ultimately gives you greater confidence in your decision-making.

7. **Feel self-compassion.** With this type of awareness, you love and accept yourself as you are without self-blame or criticism.

MEDITATION PAYOFFS

Mindfulness meditation will help you weather your financial ups and downs, as well as cultivate more confidence, initiative, and resourcefulness. You'll learn how to:

1. Pay attention in a particular way.
2. Alert and focus your attention.
3. Dismiss distractions and direct your thoughts.
4. Monitor and redirect problematic emotions.
5. Facilitate and improve brainstorming.
6. Identify new ideas and capture them.
7. Be more creative.
8. Focus your thoughts and create specific goals.
9. Stay on target to get it done.

Engaging in mindfulness meditation means you are creating intention and motivation for your mind to alter the way it perceives, receives, and reacts to thoughts and emotions. Practicing mindfulness meditation on a regular basis (once or twice daily is best) brings a sense of equanimity to what is happening moment to moment, training your mind and your brain to observe and embrace (or deflect) anything and everything that makes its way into your mind—and you learn to do this without judgment, with acceptance and openness to what is happening in your mind.

NO WAITING, START TODAY!

According to Buddhist master Sakyong Mipham Rinpoche, the easiest way to begin a mindfulness meditation practice is to meditate twice a day for short periods of time: ten, fifteen, or twenty minutes each. Luckily, you can practice mindfulness meditation in the comfort of your home or anywhere else, by creating a physical and mental space that you can claim as your own for ten minutes twice a day. Later you may want to practice for longer or participate in guided meditations. Following are the basic guidelines for practicing mindfulness meditation.

Step #1: Create a Space for Wealth

To calm and center your mind, you need privacy, peace, and quiet. If you have spiritual talismans and their presence lends itself to your practice, by all means have them nearby and integrate them into the quieting of your mind and spirit. Some people like to focus on a small talisman that they put on the floor in front of them. Why not use whatever symbol of wealth speaks to you, such as a gold coin or a model of the car you'd like to drive or gemstones that represent prosperity, like jade?

Step #2: Sit Up Straight

Buddhists believe that energy flows best when your body is sitting erectly. You can achieve the desired position by balancing on a somewhat firm pillow with your hips straight and your legs crossed. If you need to sit on a chair, sit up straight with your feet flat on the floor. Place your hands, palm upward, on your thighs. Some people like to touch their index fingers and thumbs together, but whatever feels comfortable and receptive is fine.

Step #3: Inhabit Your Body

Once you are in the correct posture, it's easier to bring your full attention to your body and your mind. Before you meditate, visualize that you have a string running from the base of your spine that you are using to slowly pull each vertebra upward into alignment. When you reach the top of your head, your shoulders and hips should both be level on the pillow or cushion, and you should feel fully present in your body. Ideally, you will feel relaxed but awake. Sleepiness is not the goal, as mindfulness meditation is all about training your mind.

Step #4: Minimize Distractions

If you want to play music during your mindfulness meditation, choose something soothing that relaxes rather than excites your mind. As you progress, you may want to experiment with guided meditations (those led by a taped voice), or you could even create an individualized guided meditation. For strict mindfulness practice, keep your eyes open but with your gaze softened (slightly out of focus) and your line of sight facing down, focusing no more than a couple of inches in front of your nose. This helps you achieve the desired containment of your mind. If you have trouble minimizing your focus, try putting a small object on the ground in front of you. Use it to refocus whenever your mind wanders.

Step #5: Breathe in Abundance, Breathe Out Scarcity

Controlling your breath is also very helpful in slowing your body down and focusing your mind. Begin by focusing solely on your breath, neither forcing nor exaggerating your breaths, just noticing as each breath enters and exits your body. As you breathe in and out normally, consciously use the motion of the breaths to relax your body and your mind. If you're a shallow breather who rarely breathes from your diaphragm, ease your way into taking slower and deeper breaths. Placing a hand on your bellybutton, so your can feel your belly rise and fall as you breathe in and out, will help you learn to breathe more deeply.

Let It Be

It's fairly typical to have upward of 300 thoughts in one thirty-minute session of mindfulness meditation—which is why it's so challenging to ignore them whizzing past. It's not easy to turn off the thought-generating process, but take heart in knowing that it is possible to do. Labeling your thoughts is one effective method, as long as you label and then release them, of course. Mindfulness meditation is all about staying focused on the now, on simply being. In time, you'll learn how to skillfully allow thoughts to sail in and sail out of the harbor without succumbing to their usual bid to distract you.

Step #6: Keep Your Eye on the Prize

During mindfulness meditation, you focus solely on being fully present and conscious in your body. When your thoughts wander or emotions rise up—and they will, galloping about like wild horses—take notice of where they've gone, label them ("distraction," "fodder for later thought," "the usual fear"), and then bring your mind back to the meditation. Focusing on your breath is a good way to bring your mind back to the process.

During meditation, your mind is learning a new way to slow down, relax, and perceive and process information. You are effectively training your mind to eradicate extraneous distraction and focus clearly on one thought at a time.

Insight Meditation Offers Another Option

Insight meditation teaches you to first be mindful of your inner environment, and then to expand your attention outwards—on sounds, smells, and temperature changes, and so on. This outwardly directed attention teaches you to merely experience the world, without trying to interpret it, and to keep your internal environment stable. Researchers at Massachusetts General Hospital found some indication that insight meditation increased the thickness of the gray matter around the right prefrontal cortex (your evaluative cortex) and the right insula (dedicated to your internal state). Practitioners have reported sustained attention, focus, and the ability to think before reacting to stressful or new situations. Not surprisingly, insight meditation tends to attract lawyers, businessmen, and executives.

Step #7: Cool Down

Once you have meditated for the allotted time, slowly bring your awareness back to the room. A few deep, cleansing breaths is a great way to notify your body and mind that you're transitioning from focused meditation to living in your normal world.

Meditating Brain, Mindful Brain

Amazing things are occurring in your brain as you mindfully meditate:

- Labeling your inner emotions with words activates your left PFC, which reduces anxiety. Conversely, if you focus on an outward source, such as a flickering candle, labeling those experiences will be more likely to activate your right PFC.
- Engaging your concentration alters the connection between your thinking and your emotional brain, strengthening the

neuronal pathways that are involved in higher-level thinking and control of your emotional centers, which allows for more voluntary recognition and management of emotions.

- Being fully present activates your cortical networks near your cingulate cortex (increases empathy and self-awareness), the insula (focuses on internal body states), and the somatosensory cortex (senses your body in space), making the focus on *you* and how you are feeling in relation to the world.
- Engaging in self-observation and awareness activates the middle PFC (your center of metacognition, where thinking about thinking or evaluating one's own reasoning occurs).

Obviously, all of these brain benefits will serve you well in your quest for wealth.

RAMP UP THOSE THETA WAVES

The more brain systems fire synchronously, the better your mental health. Mindfulness meditation practiced on a regular basis will increase left frontal lobe activity and lower emotional reactivity, as well as help you (and your brain) become more self-observant, positive, and compassionate. Mindfulness meditation tunes up brain circuitry and connects the social circuits of mirror neurons that recognize emotional faces in others and help you identify what others feel. It does this by improving self-awareness, cultivating your sense of empathy for yourself, and improving your ability to regulate and consciously express your emotions. Mindfulness and insight meditation also ramp up those elusive theta waves—the ones that are interested in emotions—and tune them with alpha and gamma waves, giving that elusive sense of "bliss" often described by practitioners.

INTEGRATING MINDFULNESS MEDITATION INTO YOUR LIFE

The more you practice mindfulness meditation, the more you will find the process both relaxing and rejuvenating. You may soon also find yourself corralling your mind and living fully present and conscious in your everyday life.

Once you know how to mindfully meditate, all you have to do is pause throughout your day (or when you're awake at night) to drop in. You can simply take meaningful pauses to breathe deeply in and out and to focus, however briefly, on being fully present in the moment. If you make dropping in to see how you're doing a habit, you will build a mindfulness muscle that will help you stay fully attentive to your intentions and your process.

INCORPORATING MINDFULNESS

Once you've mastered mindfulness meditation, the next step is living mindfully. Granted, trying to live mindfully is not an easy skill to master. It's all too easy to let your daily routines, your habits, and your thoughts swallow your best intentions. Unfortunately, this leaves you feeling disconnected from what is happening around you . . . or even within your own body. Living mindfully involves paying attention to everything that happens within your body and around you in the present moment—without judgment. It means remaining conscious instead of falling sway to your usual patterns of thinking and acting, or, more appropriately, reacting.

Your brain was designed to categorize and evaluate everything that you think, see, hear, feel, taste, or smell, but unless you are consciously piloting your brain, your brain can veer off course and get lost in all those habitual thoughts. So, work on training your brain to be focused on your current reality via meditation or mindfulness meditation, and get those neuronal paths cleared for liftoff.

Living Mindfully Technique #1: Practice a Mini-Meditation

Several times a day, stop whatever you are doing, close your eyes, and focus on your breath until your mind quiets. As thoughts arise, allow them to float away by gently redirecting your mind back to your inhalations and exhalations, blotting out whatever is going on around you. Stay in the "mini-meditation" for five minutes and work your way up to fifteen minutes. With practice, you can easily learn to quiet any mind chatter that may have been distracting you. It's a great way to refocus when your mind has been wandering.

Living Mindfully Technique #2: Be Fully Present

You can also practice mindfulness by being fully conscious of and engaged in what you choose to do at each moment. For example, if you are chopping carrots for your salad, bring your full attention to the task. Cease all external and internal conversation and focus on the sharpness of the knife blade as it slices into the meaty carrot, the sound of your knife scraping the pieces across the cutting board, the texture and taste of a slice when you pop it into your mouth.

As you will quickly see, mindfulness can be very effective in drowning out distractions and quieting an overactive mind, plus it helps your brain focus on the enjoyment of each experience.

The more you practice these simple techniques, particularly if you reinforce them by meditating mindfully, the more you'll train your brain to do whatever needs to be done, in the most efficient way possible, to accumulate wealth.

HOW LIVING AND MEDITATING MINDFULLY CAN LEAD TO GREATER WEALTH

When it comes to generating wealth, training your brain to be more observant, more tuned-in to others, and more optimistic will allow you to evaluate opportunities more rationally and logically. You will also be able to judge the person in charge of those opportunities and to make thoughtful decisions (even when your emotions are running high).

Mindfulness meditation and living mindfully will also help you train your brain to minimize distractions and to focus on subjects that you choose, when you choose to do so. Being able to calm your brain will help you focus and free up the neurons required for evaluative analysis.

Mindfulness meditation in essence rewires your brain so that you break the pattern of responding to new stimuli and experiences automatically. The point of meditation is not to stop you from having an emotional response to what's happening in your life, but to avoid responding purely out of habit. This could prove invaluable in dealing with investment anxiety. It can also simply help you cope when finances are running a bit tight so that you don't make foolish, fear-based mistakes. It will stop you from acting in the same way you always have and will instead allow you to react thoughtfully, even if you experience fear, anxiety, worry, or frustration. Mindfulness reminds you that when it comes to your reactions, you're the one in charge.

Thus, by establishing a daily practice of meditation, you are magnifying your brain's ability to function at peak capacity and grow, both of which are crucial to creating and generating wealth. So grab your favorite pillow, sit yourself down, and breathe in and out. . . .

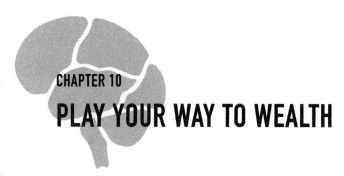

CHAPTER 10

PLAY YOUR WAY TO WEALTH

Principle: Your brain needs periods of stimulation and periods of relaxation—and it loves to learn new skills.

Playful activities stimulate unused portions of your brain, create new synapses, prevent you from being stuck in neuronal ruts, provide valuable stress relief, and make you happier (and a happier person tends to make more money!). Playing is a formidable tool in reducing stress, and offers your brain the all-important breathing space we mentioned in Chapter 8. Also, creativity has been positively linked to an ability to play. If that's not enough to get you psyched up to play, you're not having enough fun.

THE IMPORTANCE OF PLAY

There's a reason kids look so happy. It's because they're allowed— even encouraged—to play . . . and most adults are not. Play remains critical to your brain health throughout your life—and vitally important as you age. Play helps create a healthier, happier, more highly functioning brain. Playing is fun, and a great stress reliever, but it also stimulates your mind and keeps your brain supple. So, how do you feel about play?

1. **You play hooky:**
   A. Once a month.
   B. Once a quarter.
   C. Once a year.
   D. You've never played hooky.

2. **You have sex:**
   A. at least three times a week.
   B. once a week.
   C. once a month.
   D. You can't remember the last time you had sex.

3. **Your idea of mental challenge would be:**
   A. learning to speak a new language.
   B. mastering *The New York Times* crossword puzzle.
   C. beating every level of the latest video game.
   D. watching "Jeopardy."

4. **You'd be most likely to blow a week's pay on:**
   A. a financial planning seminar.
   B. a strong stock market tip.
   C. a power suit.
   D. playing blackjack.

5. **Your idea of a physical challenge is:**
   A. training for a triathlon.
   B. taking up fencing.
   C. playing a round of golf once a month.
   D. walking to the refrigerator.

6. **You take a vacation:**
   A. Every weekend is a vacation!
   B. twice a year.
   C. once a year.
   D. What's a vacation?

7. **You love a good game of:**
   A. geocaching.
   B. bridge.
   C. solitaire.
   D. You never play games.

8. **When I want to learn something new, I:**
   A. celebrate my progress with rewards.
   B. list my goals and check them off as I achieve them.
   C. quit halfway through the process.
   D. wait until the feeling passes.

Answer Key

If you checked mostly As, you have made play a part of your lifestyle, but you can still allow yourself to play harder—and reap the benefits.

If you checked mostly Bs, you occasionally indulge yourself in play, but you need to make more time in your life for fun, to give your brain the recess time it needs to foster creativity and boost your productivity.

If you checked mostly Cs, you have forgotten how good it feels to play. You are undoubtedly bored, and possibly stressed out. You need to get out and have some fun, for your bank account's sake, as well as your body and your brain's sake.

If you checked mostly Ds, you are missing out on life's greatest pleasures. All work and no play is dulling your life—and destroying your potential for financial success. Get out there and have some fun before you go completely broke.

PLAYING WITH YOUR BRAIN

As we discussed in Chapter 1, the greater your positive energy, the more money you're likely to make. Playing not only stimulates your brain's pleasure centers, it replenishes your brain, sparks creativity, and helps your mind relax. Basically, playful activity stimulates your brain to think—and feel—that this is fun! To maximize enjoyment and reinforce the good feelings, your brain starts pumping out that neurotransmitter that we love so much: dopamine. But that's not all: Your brain also supplies the feel-good chemicals oxytocin, vaso-pressin, and endorphins. A happy brain is a wealthy brain.

The upshot is that your brain goes on a badly needed holiday. Obviously, the more pleasurable experiences you create, the happier and more energized you'll be—as long as you don't succumb to addictions or excessive irresponsibility.

We're all for playing your way to greater wealth, so let's begin.

NOVELTY PAYS OFF IN SPADES

As we've discussed throughout this book, introducing your brain to new experiences helps it form new neuronal pathways. And the more you do something, the more synapses your brain fires and creates. Novelty is great because it will stimulate synapses that have lain dormant or create entirely new ones. Keep in mind that your brain adapts and grows to process and understand whatever it is that you deem important.

Music: A Mind-Altering Substance

Researcher Dr. Charles Limb at the National Institutes of Health used fMRI to scan the brains of professional jazz musicians while they were making improvisational, spur-of-the moment piano recordings. His research group found that improvisation (compared to produced replication of overlearned musical sequences) was consistently characterized by the deactivation of the lateral areas of the PFC, which assist with "tamping down" behaviors, and with abnormally high activation of the medial PFC. This unique neural pattern offered a glimpse into the cognitive context that enables the emergence of spontaneous creative activity, i.e., this study examined the font of creativity and the unique expression of the self, something jazz musicians know a thing or two about.

One reason why play is so valuable is that it exposes you to new experiences and breaks your brain out of its usual ruts. One way to play is to try something new.

- If you're athletic, try something that will flex your brain more than your biceps, like learning to design your own website.
- If you're obsessive day-trader, try learning table tennis (which is great for your brain because it involves anticipation, memory, analysis, and physical coordination, all at a very rapid pace).
- If you haven't balanced your checkbook in five years, try taking an astronomy class and memorizing the constellations.
- If you've had the same job for more than ten years, take skydiving lessons and learn to take a leap.

It doesn't matter *what* you do as long as you do something that will engage and challenge your brain. Picking something you find intriguing or joyful will strengthen your resolve to keep doing it—but you won't know how much you like it until you try it. We'll get you started by listing activities known to be good stimulators for brain growth, but once you get the hang of it, make up a list of things you would enjoy that would limber up your brain and enhance your prosperity.

NOVEL IDEAS FOR STIMULATING YOUR BRAIN

Learning a new skill boosts your happiness level—even when the process is challenging—and happiness boosts your ability to generate more wealth, whether it's monetarily, emotionally, spiritually, or any other way. According to a recent San Francisco State University study, people who master a competency—from mathematics to driving a car—experience increased feelings of happiness and satisfaction, no matter how hard-won that mastery may have proven. Any activity you enjoy will make you happier, but we suggest you also take up activities that will stimulate brain activity, and here are a few ideas to get you started:

- **Learn to read music and play a musical instrument.** Reading music and playing an instrument has consistently been shown to morph your brain in ways that few other activities can. Even listening to music has been shown to enhance your "creative process." If you're already a musician, take up sculpting or fly-fishing. You get the drift . . . challenge your mind and your coordination by doing something you've never done before, something that makes you—and your brain—grow.
- **Learn to practice origami.** The art of origami requires learning complicated patterns and an entire new "language" of folds, symbols, and patterns. It requires manual dexterity, hand/eye coordination, and a sharp eye for shapes and spatial

relationships. It's also something you can do with your children, providing hours of creative fun for all.

- **Learn to write calligraphy.** Calligraphy also involves intensive hand/eye coordination and the necessity to learn new ways of doing something you normally do without thinking at all.

- **Learn to build scale models.** Scale modeling enhances certain cognitive skills, such as concentration, visual-motor skills, and executive functions your brain uses to plan, organize, strategize, and both pay attention to and remember details. It could also inspire you to research the history related to whatever you are modeling.

- **Learn how to play complicated card games.** They provide excellent brain exercise by challenging your working memory, improving mathematical skills, improving your ability to assess calculations, risks, and odds—and they sharpen your people-reading skills. Online games are also fine, but being with people can lead to storytelling and retaining all the gossip that goes along with game playing.

Long Live Your Nerve Cells!

Nerve cells—which generate while you're still floating in your mother's uterus—can live 100 years or longer! It was once thought that nerve cells weren't replaced when they died, but recent studies show that new nerve cells can arise in a few regions of the brain, even in older brains. So it's very important to continue to stimulate your brain, not only to improve the longevity of your existing nerve cells, but also for production of new nerve cells. Your brain and body do their jobs by ensuring an ongoing process of cellular detoxification and repair, but it's up to you to provide the nurturance and stimulation required to keep your brain cells awake and alive.

PLAYING FOR FUN AND PROFIT

Since negative thinking can deflate your spirits and lead your brain astray, it only makes sense that doing things that bring you pleasure and joy can boost your spirits, lead to increased creativity, and benefit your brain. And playing is all about having fun and boosting optimism.

Pleasure Versus Enjoyment

Before you leap into joyful play, do you know the difference between pleasurable and enjoyable? Pleasure is the feeling that comes from satisfying physical needs such as hunger, sex, and bodily comfort. Enjoyment, on the other hand, derives from the good feelings you experience when you break through the limits of your body and into the realm of your thinking mind. Enjoyment comes when you:

- accomplish something that stretches your limits or breaks new ground.
- exceed your own and others' expectations (such as landing a big account, designing a new product, or building a new business).
- participate in a stimulating conversation, brainstorming session, or networking event.

Pleasure for pleasure's sake serves a purpose and is fabulous, but you also want to experience the longer-lasting enjoyment that will lead to personal and financial growth.

Ready, Set, Reward!

If you are overtaxed or chronically stressed, planning something fun is critical to your financial well-being. Enjoyment itself has a multitude of benefits, plus making time for enjoyable activities stimulates parts of the brain associated with creative and positive thinking. You become even more emotionally and intellectually motivated. Any time you take a break from routine, you develop new ways of thinking.

Avoid Brain Fog

Chronic stress kills . . . literally. Studies show that stress has disastrous physical effects, but did you know that chronic stress also diverts energy from your brain (fogs up your mind), shrinks the part of your brain associated with memory and learning, compromises neurotransmitters (limiting joy *and* plasticity), and even emits toxins that attack your brain? Forget zombies; *stress* eats your brain! Make it a priority to relax. Doing things that are physically and mentally stimulating and energizing is fine, but they also have to be relaxing—with an emphasis on fun!

To begin, make a list of five activities that stimulate your pleasure centers and five activities that bring you enjoyment. In case you need greater clarification, here are two lists to spur your creative process. The first is a list of suggestions for activities that might bring you pleasure, and the second is a list of suggestions for activities that might bring the longer-lasting feeling of enjoyment that comes from mastery.

Things that might immediately stimulate your pleasure centers:

- scoring a great deal on a valuable antique
- trying out a new recipe
- test driving a fancy sports car
- discovering a new restaurant
- romping under the sheets with your significant other

Things that might bring enjoyment (*and* stimulate your brain's quest for new experiences and learning new tasks):

- designing and building a piece of furniture
- planning a five-city tour of Europe
- auditioning for a part in a local theatre production
- attending a music camp
- learning to play golf

The important thing is to create your own lists, using your brain to come up with ideas that are both creative and surprising. Flex that imagination, fire up those brain cells, let your inner child explore, and have fun with the process and the execution. Challenge yourself to come up with fresh ideas each month and open up your mind to suggestions.

Anticipation Stimulates Your Brain

Anticipation is often sweeter than the actual experience, particularly when the upcoming event is expected to be pleasurable, such as going out on a romantic date or taking a beach vacation. *Anticipating* future rewards lights up the pleasure centers in your limbic system, especially your nucleus accumbens in the same way *experiencing* the event does. Think about it: You feel butterflies and grin endlessly an hour before that hot date. This is because your brain recognizes all of the situations leading up to the ultimate reward. So dream up something that will lead to joyful anticipation. Even if making it happen seems an impossibility, envision what you'd like to happen, in minute detail, savoring each mental picture. Remember that visualizing something intensely can trick your brain into thinking it's an actual experience. So it really is almost like being there.

As you enjoy new experiences and conquer challenges, take time to fully savor each moment. Then, on the days you're not feeling the *go-out-there-and-do-it* vibe, you can call up those memories—in detail—and give your brain the same thrilling experience all over again.

GET A HOBBY!

If you already have a hobby that you do regularly, you already know the pleasures associated with doing something just for fun. If you don't have a hobby, you need one. Hobbies offer opportunities to exercise parts of yourself that are not being tapped in your professional world, as well as ways to quiet your mind and stimulate your creativity. Some hobbies may have formed in your childhood and brought you such pleasure that you continue to do them, or you would like to continue to do them—if only you could find the time.

Finding the time to enjoy a hobby or two should be moved to the top of your list. We're all for working hard—and believe that you have to work hard to succeed—but playing hard is also important for your well-being and for maintaining maximum brain functioning. Hobbies could range from collecting Star Wars' character toys to handcrafting jewelry to refinishing furniture found at garage sales. It doesn't matter what you do, only that you *love* doing it.

Hobbies can be fabulous diversions, a way to reduce stress, and a way to create something that offers a more tangible level of fulfillment.

If you are in a job that doesn't produce something tangible, being able to complete a work of art, or create a photography exhibit, or build elaborate, fanciful birdhouses offers you an opportunity to create something you can hold in your hands and feel proud about sharing. Hobbies can lead to passion, increased social interaction, and a whole host of brain goodies. When you're really engaged in a hobby you love, you are able to access that highly desirable heightened state of concentration (known as being in the flow), which increases chemicals (such as endorphins, norepinephrine, and dopamine) that energize and restore your brain.

Additional benefits of hobbies include:

1. They stimulate new ideas and neural connections that can lead to a flurry of insights and fresh perspectives that may spark your creativity and infuse your profession in ways you cannot imagine.
2. They require commitment and focus, which create a higher level of neuronal engagement—and produce a feeling of accomplishment.
3. They activate more of your brain's real estate, some of which may never be stimulated in your chosen field.
4. They create an expanded vision of yourself, providing multiple areas where you can excel, thereby enhancing self-esteem and reducing the impact of bad days at work or a negative quarterly review.

The ideal hobby would engage your brain, engender passion, provide opportunities for an expanded social network—and offer a sense of fulfillment. Whichever hobby you choose, make sure to add intellectual components, such as researching the history of your chosen hobby, and add a social component, such as attending ballroom or country-western dancing classes, joining bird-watching or garden clubs, attending art, photography, writing, jewelry-making, knitting, or quilting classes, and so on.

If your hobby involves creating something, you can also add a spiritual component, such as donating whatever you make to homeless shelters or assisted living facilities or charity auctions, which will bring another level of enjoyment and fulfillment.

Additionally, your passionate hobby might inspire a whole new career. Legions of people ultimately shift gears—from doing something they thought they'd love but grew to hate, or from losing interest in whatever they were doing and wanting to do something that actually brought them pleasure—and fires up their creativity. More and more people decide to strike out as entrepreneurs, and passionate hobbies are often just the ticket.

SPEND QUALITY TIME WITH COLLEAGUES AND MENTORS

Humans were not designed to live—or work—alone. Nature created our brains to know that we need other people. Your brain releases internal opiates—endorphins—that create that lovely feeling you experience when near someone you value and trust. Studies have consistently shown that feeling connected, loved, and supported improves your health—and your bank account.

Harkening back to what we learned about the brain, fostering close relationships stimulates what some scientists call your social brain, including mirror neurons—those little neurons that allow you to identify with and grow closer to other humans and also allow you to mirror the qualities you admire in colleagues and mentors.

Flexing your social brain stimulates your pleasurable limbic system while quieting your fearful amygdala. In other words, it helps you tamp down anxiety and more deeply feel the connection, support, and encouragement that can make you even more successful.

PROFIT FROM ORGASM

You might think of sex as being something that primarily makes your body feel good, but it's oh-so-good for your brain—and your bank account, too!

Bring on the Dopamine!
It doesn't take a neuroscientist to figure out that good sex creates a physical and emotional high. Many areas of your brain are

involved in creating and processing the pleasure from sex, but there are three major ones:

1. When you're engaged in flirting, foreplay, and the ultimate act of sex itself, your ventral tegmental area (VTA) is spilling out dopamine at a mile a minute, most of which makes its way to the limbic area called the nucleus accumbens. This nucleus is at the seat of both seeking and enjoying pleasure; it's active when you're pursuing the act of sex and also enjoying the fruits of your labor.
2. That big boost of dopamine in the accumbens is what makes you feel great, and makes you crave more and more sensation.
3. The dopamine from your VTA also causes signals to go to your PFC so that you understand *why* and *how* you're getting to have all this great fun!

An orgasm provides the biggest blast of legal, naturally occurring dopamine available to your brain. Dutch researchers, after scanning the brains of lucky volunteers experiencing orgasm, likened their brain scans to scans of people experiencing heroin rushes! Not only do you get that huge rush of stimulating neurotransmitters, but orgasm may also release a rush of oxytocin (also known as the "love hormone"), especially in women. Oxytocin cements a strong social connection bond with the person closest to you when orgasm was achieved. It also brings that sense of euphoric calm after orgasm and is key in relieving stress, which, as you now know, is a brain killer.

Oxytocin also works as a neuromodulator, which means it sensitizes your body's response to endorphins, which often act as natural painkillers, particularly for headaches. Yes, that's right, having sex can *cure* headaches.

The more sex you have on a regular basis, the more your blood circulation improves, which helps keep your body healthy and functioning overall, and keeps you—and your brain—youthful. Sex is great exercise! If you're not in the mood, take a minute to envision how good it will feel to have oxytocin and dopamine lubricating, nourishing, and regenerating your neurons.

God and Money

Having an orgasm can be a religious experience—or at least as close to one as some may get. Researchers in Finland stumbled on this juicy bit of information while researching blood flow and activity patterns in the brain. Rather inadvertently, they discovered that a religious experience and having an orgasm both light up the outside of the right temporal lobe— what some scientists refer to as your "god area." Hallelujah!

LAUGH ALL THE WAY TO THE BANK

Scientists have found that three parts of your brain light up when you laugh. Your PFC responds, and helps you grasp the meaning behind the joke; the supplementary motor cortex tells your facial muscles to move; and areas of your limbic circuit like the hippocampus and the amygdala elicit that delicious giddy feeling. Laughing simply feels good, although what makes us laugh and why remains mysterious. Sometimes it's cultural and/or weirdly personal. John Morreall, a humor researcher at the College of William and Mary, notes that laughter is "a playful response to incongruities, involving stories that disobey conventional expectations." So laughter is a little bit naughty—and loads of fun.

Laughter also lets those around us know when we are purposefully lightening up, and usually indicates that we want them to laugh, too. (If we're lucky, their mirror neurons will kick in and respond accordingly.) In the end, it doesn't matter why or how or when we laugh, all laughter will make you feel better—if only for a moment.

Laughing also has amazing health benefits. It beats back the tide of stress hormones (cortisol, in particular), giving your body a healthy break; it lowers blood pressure, reducing the risk of blood clots; it strengthens your immune system; and it generates the release of endorphins, the body's natural high.

Get Your Smile On!

Studies have shown that a baby smiles 400 times a day, children up to preschool age laugh about 300 times a day, and adults laugh an average of fifteen times a day. Research has shown that the mere act of smiling can lighten your mood. If you're feeling down, take a walk around your office and smile at your coworkers. Before long someone will tell a funny story and you'll all feel better.

THE FUN'S NOT OVER

We hope this chapter inspired you to make room for having a lot more pleasurable fun in your life, not only to cheer you up, but also to stimulate and keep your brain young. Next, we'll discuss the importance of exercise, which plays a critical role in brain health and function.

CHAPTER 11

EXERCISE YOUR WAY TO WEALTH

Principle: Your brain is a bodily organ dependent upon you to do what it takes to keep it healthy and that includes keeping your body in shape and the bloodlines flowing.

We all know exercise is extremely good for our overall health and well-being, but exercising (particularly aerobic exercise) plays a vital role in your quest for wealth because it:

- stimulates circulation and increases blood flow to all parts of your body and brain, which keeps your brain well nourished, youthful, receptive, flexible, and finely tuned.
- increases healthy growth factors in the memory center of your brain.
- involves coordination between your muscles which helps your brain think faster and better.
- increases self-esteem and confidence, which is worth its weight in gold.

TURN AN EYE TO EXERCISE

Now that you're clear on the role exercise plays in creating a super-healthy, super-efficient brain, let's see how well you're doing exercise-wise.

The *Exercise for Abundance* Quiz

1. **You do thirty minutes or more of exercise:**
   - **A.** five days a week.
   - **B.** three times a week.
   - **C.** twice a month.
   - **D.** never.

2. **Your idea of perfect exercise is:**
   - **A.** training for a marathon with your best friend.
   - **B.** a pickup game of basketball with your colleagues.
   - **C.** a walk around the block.
   - **D.** a nap.

3. **When you're pressed for time, you:**
   - **A.** get up an hour earlier to go to the gym.
   - **B.** squeeze in an exercise video.
   - **C.** skip working out until your schedule calms down.
   - **D.** happily cross exercise off your to-do list.

4. **You think of exercise as:**
   - **A.** fun.
   - **B.** critical to your health.
   - **C.** a necessary evil.
   - **D.** the last thing you'd ever want to do.

Answer Key

If you responded with "C" or "D" answers, you may need to rethink your relationship with exercise. If you want to build wealth, one way to do it is by building muscle!

USE YOUR NOGGIN

Researchers at the University of California–Irvine have demonstrated that the changes that take place in your brain as a result of exercise (including the growth of neural connections) occur because exercise stimulates certain types of genes known as *neural growth factors*. One of these genes, affectionately called "noggin," may be important in helping to prevent or curtail the onset of Alzheimer's disease, since neural growth factors contribute to strengthening your memory.

Scientists at Northwestern University have also recently found that particularly vigorous exercise slows down the production of a protein (bone morphogenic protein, or BMP) that interferes with the production of new neurons and neural growth factors. Thus, vigorous exercise means less BMP, which is a good thing. Exercise helps you keep your brain nimble and active, both when you're young and as you get older.

As long as your physical activity of choice is not endangering your skull, all exercise is good for your brain, and with consistent, moderate exercise, your brain will do whatever you need it to do.

And Let's Not Forget Stress Relief!

Exercise, particularly playful exercise, is one of nature's most potent stress relievers. Your body and your brain need times when you're not intently focused, burning up the neurons, or worrying about outcomes. Since it is a well-known fact that business decisions made under stress often have extremely negative consequences, any activity that creates less stress on brain functioning will positively enhance financial decision-making.

Age-Proof Your Brain

The effects of exercise on your brain never cease. In fact, as you get older, exercise becomes even *better* for your overall brain health. Neuroscientists have shown that in aging populations (usually those over age sixty-five), sustained, moderate exercise participation enhances learning and memory, improves the function of the insightful brain, counteracts age-related and disease-related mental decline, and protects against age-related atrophy in brain areas crucial for thinking and learning. Exercise has been cited by several researchers, including those at the University of California–Irvine, as being the number one factor in sustaining brain health and the ability to make new neurons in an aging brain.

Double Your Benefits

Best of all, it doesn't even matter what kind of exercise you choose (although aerobic exercise that gets your heart pumping is best). As long as you move your body regularly, it will boost your brain's ability to function. But if you pick something you love doing, you'll be stimulating your pleasure centers at the same time, and those neural links between pleasure and exercise will reinforce your will to exercise even more! Here are some ideas:

- Join a running club
- Hike through the woods
- Sign up for a 5-K or 10-K race
- Take up crewing
- Learn martial arts

- Try Pilates
- Work with a personal trainer
- Take a ballroom dancing class
- Walk your dogs on a beach
- Go on a bike tour

Thirty Is the Magic Number

U.S. federal guidelines for exercise say that getting at least thirty minutes a day most days a week will help prevent heart disease, osteoporosis, diabetes, obesity, and, perhaps, Alzheimer's disease. Brisk walking for thirty minutes a day is all that is needed for brain health—and it doesn't have to be thirty consecutive minutes. You can walk briskly for ten minutes three times a day, or for five minutes six times a day.

Get a Dog!

A Michigan State University study of the exercise habits of 5,900 people, including 2,170 who owned dogs, found that about two-thirds of dog owners took their pets for regular walks, lasting for at least ten minutes. Among dog owners who took their pets for regular walks, 60 percent met federal criteria for regular moderate or vigorous exercise. Nearly half exercised an average of thirty minutes a day at least five days a week. By comparison, only about a third of those without dogs got that much regular exercise.

They also found that the dog walkers had higher overall levels of both moderate and vigorous physical activity than the other subjects—and they were more likely to enjoy and take part in other physical activities, such as sports and gardening. On average, they exercised about thirty minutes a week more than people who didn't have dogs.

A study of 41,500 California residents found that dog owners were about 60 percent more likely to walk for leisure than people who owned a cat, or no pet at all. That translated to an extra 19 minutes a week of walking compared with people without dogs.

The Burden of Belly Fat

That bulge around your middle, a.k.a. the dreaded belly fat, also lodges unseen visceral fat around your heart and other vital organs, and it eventually takes on a life of its own. That's right: Belly fat cells are capable of producing their own hormones, and they release cytokines, the same inflammatory chemicals that your body releases when it needs to ward off an infection or heal from an injury. These cytokines have been linked to depression, decreased ability for long-term memory, and may lower your brain's plasticity.

In a twelve-week study of fifty-four older adults at an assisted-living home, researchers at the University of Missouri showed that dogs make better walking companions than humans. Some participants selected a friend or spouse as a walking companion, while others took a bus daily to a local animal shelter, where they were assigned a dog to walk. Walking speed among the dog walkers increased by 28 percent, compared with just 4 percent among the human walkers. Dr. Johnson, the study's lead author, and co-author of *Walk a Hound, Lose a Pound*, noted that human walkers often complained about the heat and talked each other out of exercise, but that people who were paired with dogs didn't make those excuses.

If that's not enough to motivate you, dogs also make great companions and loving pets, and they have health benefits beyond those associated with exercise. For example, Dr. Karen Allen recently studied forty-eight stockbrokers diagnosed with hypertension. Those with pets at home had their resting systolic blood pressure elevate to only 126 during a stressful situation, while the petless groups had a much larger increase to 148. Further, Dr. Blair Justice from the University of Texas has shown that playing with a dog for just ten minutes will stimulate the release of dopamine and serotonin—and who ever gets enough of those miraculous chemicals?

BRIBE YOUR BRAIN

If you have a problem motivating yourself to exercise, we have the perfect solution—trick your mind to fall in love with exercise. Even if you harbor a thousand negative connotations to exercise and (like most of us) have failure etched into every memory associated with exercising, we have an ingenious, brain-specific solution: Reward your brain instead!

Wire Your Brain for Pleasure

For instance, let's say you're starting a new exercise routine, something you've attempted and failed to achieve many times before. To create new neuronal pathways that will support rather than diminish your will to succeed, consciously use your mind to pair up the new activity with something you consider rewarding. It could be hanging out with your colleagues after a golf tournament, meeting your coworkers at a sports bar to watch a game after your big workout, going out for tea with your tennis partner after a rousing game of doubles. Whatever you choose, make it something that brings a *genuine* feeling of pleasure to you, and keep it up! Do it the second, third, and fourth time you exercise as well.

Importantly, the reward should take place during, or immediately after, the activity. Rewarding yourself will link the new activity with positive associations and good consequences, thus reinforcing new, more positive brain connections. Soon you'll be thinking of this particular form of exercise as something you love to do, and you won't need that original reward anymore in order to feel just as good.

Put Your Brain in Neutral

Likewise, if you want to train your brain to abandon negative habits, either teach your brain to consider these habits neutral (avoid linking the negative behavior or thoughts with rewards or punishments) or teach your brain to associate them with bad circumstances (punishments).

For example, instead of getting yourself worked up over the fact that you blew half your paycheck on a new suit, don't attach negative or positive action, thought, or emotion. Neutralize it.

Demonize Bad Habits

If that doesn't work for you, the next time you blow your budget, force yourself to do something unpleasant, such as scrubbing your toilet, paying bills, or listening to heavy metal music at a ridiculously high volume. Whatever it is, it should be something that you genuinely dislike, and you should force yourself to do it every time you overspend. Soon enough, overspending will not seem worth the hassle, and you will abandon the habit.

The more your mind controls your emotions and thoughts in regard to undesirable habits, the more your brain will diminish the neuronal connections that led you down the same old path. Associating certain kinds of thoughts with no meaning, no reward, and no punishment will eventually extinguish those thoughts.

TIRED FROM ALL THAT EXERCISE?

If that workout has left you worn out, don't worry. The next chapter covers how sleep can help your brain create new riches.

CHAPTER 12

SLEEP YOUR WAY TO WEALTH

Principle: Restorative sleep is vital to your brain's ability to grow and function at peak capacity.

You can play, you can exercise regularly, and you can stimulate those little gray cells, but if you don't get enough sleep, wealth may still elude you. Why? Because sleep rejuvenates your brain and is essential to your brain's ability to make new and stronger connections, to integrate information, and to function at peak capacity. Achieving wealth, as it turns out, is often a matter of catching some Zzzzs.

COUNTING SHEEP?

Let's begin by evaluating the quality and quantity of the rest you receive each night—the rest that's so critical to your money-making brain.

The *Nap Time Is Money* Quiz

1. **Each night you sleep an average of:**
   A. seven and a half hours or more.
   B. six to seven hours.
   C. four to six hours.
   D. Sleep? Who needs sleep?

2. **You take a thirty-minute nap:**
    A. every day.
    B. three or four days a week.
    C. Saturday and/or Sunday afternoons.
    D. Naps? Those are for losers.

3. **Every night in preparation for bed, you:**
    A. crawl under the covers and are asleep within minutes.
    B. read in bed until you fall asleep, usually within the hour.
    C. fall asleep watching TV on the couch.
    D. lie awake for hours trying to fall asleep.

4. **You're usually asleep by:**
    A. 9 P.M.
    B. midnight.
    C. 2 A.M.
    D. dawn.

5. **You think of a good night's sleep as:**
    A. critical to your health and well-being.
    B. something you know you need but don't get.
    C. a necessary evil.
    D. an impossible dream.

6. **When you dream, you:**
    A. write them down in your dream journal upon awakening.
    B. forget them, unfortunately—you think they were cool!
    C. have nightmares and wake up screaming.
    D. You never dream.

7. **You suffer from:**
    A. no sleep disorders.
    B. restless legs syndrome.
    C. chronic insomnia.
    D. sleep apnea and/or narcolepsy.

8. **When the alarm rings in the morning, you:**
    A. turn it off and roll out of bed, raring to go.
    B. turn it off and lie there until you're more fully awake.
    C. hit the snooze button and go back to sleep—more than once.
    D. sleep through the alarm because you were up half the night.

Answer Key

If you checked mostly As, you understand the importance of sleep and strive to get enough of it. But there are still ways you can better harness the power of sleep to boost your creativity, increase your productivity, and enhance your prosperity.

If you checked mostly Bs, you get almost enough sleep to function at your peak, but never quite enough. Reviewing your sleep habits will allow you to improve your sleep patterns, giving your brain the rest it needs to bolster your performance and help you achieve your goals.

If you checked mostly Cs, you are sleep deprived, along with 40 percent of the American public. Such sleep deprivation adversely affects your health and wealth, often in ways you're not even aware of.

If you checked mostly Ds, you number among the 70 million Americans who suffer from sleep disorders—sabotaging virtually every aspect of your waking life.

THE THREE RS OF SLEEP

Sleep is your body's time to restore, renew, and reorganize itself—from head to toe. While you sleep, your cells mend, your energy replenishes, your mood stabilizes, your brain repairs, and your health optimizes. To realize the most benefit, you need to sleep seven and a half to nine hours each night. This allows your body to alleviate the damage caused by stress, ultraviolet rays, and other harmful environmental exposures.

Also, your cells produce more protein while you're sleeping than when you're awake—and you need these protein molecules to help your other cells repair and recharge. In addition, adequate sleep allows all of your body systems to regroup and reboot, which boosts your energy level upon awakening and helps carry you through your day.

A good night's sleep gives your entire system a boost. If you get fewer than seven and a half hours a night, you:

1. run the risk of high blood pressure and cholesterol, which may explain why heart attacks and strokes occur more often in the early morning hours.
2. may send your body into high-alert mode, which causes your blood pressure and your stress hormones to spike. The longer you go without enough sleep, the worse this state of hyper-arousal grows. Chronic insomnia leads to sustained hyper-arousal of your body's stress response system.
3. increase the level of stress hormones and inflammation in your body, which increases your risk for heart disease, cancer, diabetes, and—you guessed it—premature aging.
4. are more likely to be overweight or obese. The hormones ghrelin and leptin, important players in regulating appetite, are disrupted by lack of sleep.

LOSE SLEEP, LOSE MONEY

If you're not getting a good night's rest, you are sabotaging your financial security because it creates:

- Fatigue, lethargy, and lack of motivation
- Moodiness and irritability
- Reduced creativity and problem-solving skills
- Inability to cope with stress
- Concentration and memory problems
- Difficulty making decisions

In short, a sleep-deprived you is a sluggish, cranky, forgetful, indecisive, ineffective, unhappy, stressed-out you—*not* an efficient, moneymaking you. On the other hand, a well-rested you is an energetic, cheerful, creative, capable, cooperative, mellow you—a you that is ready to face the challenges of the day and take new wealth-creating opportunities as they come.

FOCUS YOUR BRAIN ON SLEEP

It's not just your body that needs sleep; it's your brain as well. Sleep is essential to your healthy brain functioning, affecting genetic processes, protein synthesis, and myelin formation. (Neurons require myelin to transmit messages quickly over long distances.) In fact, recent discoveries have revealed that sleep allows new neurons to grow in your hippocampus, the part of the brain that regulates long-term memory and spatial navigation. Adequate restful sleep also improves your brain's ability to focus, learn new skills, and remember important information.

The Consequences of Severe Sleep Deprivation

Lack of adequate, restful sleep can have immediate and devastating effects for your brain. Although it's highly unlikely that you'll literally go crazy if you don't get enough sleep, it is worth noting that sleeping problems occur in almost all people with mental disorders, including those with depression and schizophrenia.

Extreme sleep deprivation can lead to a seemingly psychotic state of paranoia and hallucinations, even in otherwise healthy people. Disrupted sleep can trigger episodes of mania, agitation, and hyperactivity. What constitutes severe sleep deprivation? Not sleeping for three or four days, or sleeping erratically over an extended period of time.

Could Night Owls Really Be Wiser?

You've heard the adage "early to bed, early to rise, makes a man healthy, wealthy, and wise." Well, a study at Stanford University and the University of Wisconsin identified a specific gene whose variations appear to turn that idea on its head. A study of 420 Air Force recruits found that cognitive ability was positively correlated with night owls and negatively correlated with early birds. Research has also shown that it's better to stay up late to finish a project than it is to get up early, as it goes against your body's desire to sleep a full eight hours and leaves you trying to work when your brain is not yet fully functional.

Even moderate sleep deprivation may slow down your brain, prevent neurons from regenerating and firing properly, limit the formation of new synapses, prevent the plasticity that allows your brain to learn new tasks, and impair memory.

COUNTING YOUR MONEY WHILE YOU SLEEP

While most of us won't go more than one night without at least some sleep, far too many of us don't get an optimum amount of sleep each night. According to the National Institutes of Health, the average adult sleeps fewer than seven hours per night. Given that we're supposed to get seven and a half to nine hours of sleep a night, this means we are a nation of sleep-deprived citizens.

If you're a working parent, a full seven hours of sleep a night might sound ideal—if only you could manage it. But even that is not enough. While sleep requirements vary slightly from person to person, most healthy adults need this seven and a half to nine hours per night to function at their best. Why? Because this is the time your body needs to downshift into dreamland, where your brain goes into overdrive.

THE BLUEPRINT FOR SLEEP

When you fall asleep, you cycle through these five stages every 90 to 110 minutes, with the deep restorative sleep and REM sleep playing the most crucial roles. These stages are:

Stage 1: **Transition to sleep,** which lasts about five minutes. Eye movement slows down, along with muscle activity.

Stage 2: **Light sleep,** which lasts ten to twenty-five minutes. This stage is characterized by slower brain waves punctuated by infrequent surges of accelerated brain waves.

Stages 3 and 4: **Deep, restorative (slow-wave) sleep,** which shortens as the night progresses. The deepest stage of sleep, this slow-wave sleep features extremely slow brain waves. During this phase, blood flow is directed away from the brain and toward the muscles, and the synthesis of protein increases.

Stage 5: **REM sleep** first occurs seventy to ninety minutes after falling asleep. This is the dreaming phase, when the focus is on brain restoration. Eyes move rapidly, breathing is shallow, arms and legs are temporarily paralyzed, and heart rate and blood pressure increase. Increased protein production occurs. The length of time spent in REM becomes longer as the night progresses.

Always Be Prepared

Much research has been done on slow-wave and REM sleep and how they benefit making memories and bolstering learning. However, until recently, little research has been conducted about the initial stages of sleep and what role they play—and it's actually a very important role. In studying rats in the early stages of sleep, Harvard Medical School researchers recently showed that their levels of adenosine triphosphate (ATP), the energy currency of cells, dramatically increased in four key brain regions (normally active during wakefulness)—especially in the frontal cortex. These results suggest that a surge of energy occurring in the early sleep stages may replenish brain processes needed to function normally while awake. Thus, if your brain doesn't progress through the preparatory sleep stages, it spends its day constantly scrambling for energy. So be a good sleep scout by easing your brain through the initial sleep stages, thereby preparing it for the next day's work.

In the beginning of the night, you spend more time in Stages 3 and 4 of sleep (i.e., slow-wave sleep) and less time in REM sleep; however, as the hours pass, you shift out of deep restorative (slow-wave) sleep and into having more REM sleep. (Slow-wave sleep prepares your brain for REM sleep.) In the hours before waking, you're spending almost all of your time in stages 1, 2, and REM sleep, with only brief passes into deep, restorative sleep.

Restore Your Body

During the slow-wave or deep restorative phase, the focus is on your body, which gets busy conducting all the restorative work that keeps it functioning optimally. Slow-wave sleep also paves the way for REM-stage sleep to replenish and renew your brain.

Restore Your Brain

During the REM phase, the focus is on your brain. Your breathing grows shallow, your muscle activity slows, and your heart and blood pressure increase, all of which help your brain take center stage. Learning and memory are intricately connected—making REM sleep critical to both. A Rockefeller University study involving rats showed that certain brain cells that are activated while we're awake tend to reactivate during REM sleep—helping us remember what we've learned during the day.

During REM sleep, your brain:

1. Consolidates and processes any and all information you've learned during the day.
2. Forms neural connections that strengthen and firm memories.
3. Replenishes its supply of neurotransmitters, including chemicals such as serotonin and dopamine. These chemicals help all parts of the brain to stay on track—neither too fast nor too slow—allowing the brain as a whole to hum along, doing the best job it can.

Sleeping also increases brain connectivity or plasticity, which helps you continue learning and growing as you age.

Double Your Test Scores

Slow-wave sleep and REM sleep work hand in hand, according to a study done at the University of Massachusetts. In the study, people were asked to remember a list of word pairs (a very common memory task). Those who slept before the test did better. More important, those who had more slow-wave sleep *and* REM sleep did the best of all.

DREAM YOURSELF RICH

You typically spend more than two hours each night dreaming. In the REM phase, the pons, located at the base of your brain, sends signals to the thalamus, which relays them to the cortex, the outer layer of the brain that is responsible for learning, thinking, and organizing information. (Remember, the cortex is the part of the brain that interprets and organizes environmental information during consciousness.) Scientists believe that the cortex tries to interpret the random signals it receives from the pons and the thalamus, essentially creating a story out of fragmented brain activity.

Falling into a deep sleep fosters dreaming; dreams help your brain process what has happened throughout the day. While your body slumbers, via dreams, your brain makes connections between events, sensory input, feelings, and memories. These memory links are essential to healthy brain functioning, which improves your waking memory.

FIRST PRACTICE, THEN SLEEP

Stickgold also studied procedural or motor memory—a type of physical recollection your brain creates when you practice the violin or learn to play tennis or write calligraphy. By studying subjects (some with and some without amnesia) after playing Tetris, a popular computer game, Stickgold found that their brains recreated images of the peculiarly shaped Tetris tiles drifting down their fields of vision before they fell asleep, especially if they slept immediately after a long practice session. Even subjects with severe amnesia, who couldn't recall having played the game at all, had the same experience, which indicated that those images must have resulted from a kind of recall that is separate from factual memory. Even more importantly, all the subjects showed improvement in their Tetris scores if they slept shortly after learning or practicing a new skill—and doubling the amount of time allowed for learning did not outweigh the benefits of sleep! So if you want to learn a new skill, make sure to grab some zzzs shortly after learning or practicing it.

GET THE SLEEP YOU NEED TO GET RICH

As we've now seen, fostering deep restoration (slow-wave) sleep and REM (dreaming) sleep are both crucial to your brain's ability to process, retain, and assimilate what occurs during your waking hours. Getting enough sleep and helping your brain achieve the deeper sleep levels is highly advantageous to your ability to keep your brain pliable and functioning at its peak capacity. Here is what to do and what not to do to improve your overall sleep quality.

Your Sleep Check-List

In order to get the good night's rest so crucial to your brain (and your wealth building), you need to avoid activities that interfere with falling—and staying—asleep.

Relax

Exercising tends to stimulate cortical alertness, which is not a good thing when you want a good night's sleep. Exercise can help decrease stress, but strenuous aerobic exercise puts the nervous system in a state of moderate arousal, which is ideal for mental tasks but not for sleep. Try not to exercise within two hours of your bedtime, and if you must do strenuous exercise in the evening, try consuming a light snack containing carbohydrates and dairy products just before bedtime.

Abstain

Alcohol consumption reduces the relative amount of time spent in REM sleep. The more alcohol you consume, the less REM sleep you get and the less rested you feel in the morning. If you drink alcohol in the evening, leave at least one hour before bedtime for the alcohol to metabolize. Also, alcohol is dehydrating, so make your chaser a tall glass of water.

Eat Lightly

Eating a large meal in the evening sends your digestive system into overdrive, which will interfere with sleep, especially the deeper phases of sleep that are so crucial to your body and your brain. Also, avoid fatty and spicy foods, as both can disrupt sleep. In general, don't eat a heavy meal within four hours of your bedtime.

Mutant Sleepers

Some people insist that they function just fine on four hours of sleep, and recent research may prove their case. Although the vast majority of us cannot function well with only four hours of sleep each night, apparently some people, known by scientists as "short sleepers," have a mutation on a gene that regulates the sleep cycle. These lucky few (depending upon how you view sleep) are typically very active, high-energy types. Hing-Hui Fu, a University of California neurology professor, noted that these short sleepers often hold down two jobs, have successful careers, and enjoy diverse activities.

Stick to a Regular Bedtime Schedule

Try to get out of bed at the same time each day, even on weekends. This trains your body—and your brain—that certain times are meant for sleep and certain times are meant for wakefulness.

However, if you are chronically short of sleep, it may be wise to catch up on the weekends. Dr. David Dinges, chief of the Division of Sleep and Chronobiology at the University of Pennsylvania, led a study that showed that healthy but sleep-deprived adults benefited from one long night of sleep (ten hours). In fact, the extended sleep was enough to improve performance nearly equal to that of people who were able to get ten hours of sleep every night for a week. So having a lazy Sunday in bed is more than just a luxury; it can substantially boost your brainpower for those Monday morning meetings.

Create a Sacred Sleep Space

Moderate the temperature to somewhere between 68°F and 72°F. Close your curtains (or invest in shades) that can effectively block sunlight or streetlights. Limit noise and distraction, such as television.

Calm Yourself

Spend some time doing sleep- or relaxation-oriented activities before bed, such as meditation; relaxation exercises; slow stretches that involve deep, rhythmic breathing; or writing in a journal. Tackling a complex work project, watching a violent movie, or reading crime thrillers: not so good. Choose activities that give your mind a rest.

Create a Bedtime Ritual

Just as you may use storytelling and lullabies to help your children sleep, you can benefit from a regular nighttime ritual. Climbing into bed with your favorite (lighthearted) novel and a small cup of chamomile tea might do the trick. Whatever you choose, make it something that helps you relax and do it for ten minutes every night.

Avoid Coffee

All types of caffeine affect your ability to fall asleep and stay asleep. Coffee is the most well-known offender, but caffeine can also be found in tea, cola, chocolate, and decaffeinated coffee. Other sources of hidden caffeine are pain pills, weight-loss pills, diuretics, and cold medicine, all of which may have enough caffeine to equal one cup of coffee.

Try a Glass of Warm Milk

Milk products stimulate melatonin production, which improves sleep. Whether skim or fat, milk, like complex carbohydrates, contains

L-tryptophan, the amino acid that is a precursor of melatonin and serotonin.

Have a Bedtime Snack

Eating a light snack may help you fall asleep. Simple sugars and fats reduce the oxygen supply to the brain, which decreases alertness and makes you sleepy. Foods that contain L-tryptophan include bananas, oats, and poultry. Yogurt and crackers or a piece of bread with a small slice of cheese are perfect bedtime snacks.

Swap Honey for Fake Sugar

If you drink a hot beverage, sweeten it with honey, sugar, or other natural flavoring. Food additives in general and artificial sweeteners in particular tend to increase alertness, and thus interfere with sleep. As a bonus, honey contains the sleep-inducing L-tryptophan.

MELLOW OUT TO BLISS OUT

The trick to sleeping soundly may be minimizing stress. If you have difficulty sleeping well at night, train your brain to mellow out in the hours leading up to bedtime.

Consider the recent Tel Aviv University study, which found that students who focused on their emotions and anxiety during high-stress periods were more likely to disrupt their sleep than those who tended to ignore their emotions and focus on tasks, effectively turning off their stress and sleeping soundly.

During a routine week of studies, and again during a highly stressful month, researchers documented the sleep patterns of thirty-six students. Sleep quality improved or remained the same for students who directed their focus away from their emotions, while sleep quality diminished for those who fretted and brooded as a way to cope with stress.

If you tend to fret and brood yourself, try to change those habits. Fretting and brooding about anything, especially about things you cannot change, is counterproductive and effectively trains your brain to go down the stress corridor.

Fifteen Minutes to Lights Out

If worrying about money, bills, or financial difficulties is keeping you awake, give yourself fifteen minutes to focus on what's bothering you—and only fifteen minutes. Spend that fifteen minutes working on three lists:

1. List all the terrible things that could go wrong: The Worst-Case Scenario
2. List all the things that might actually happen: The Realistic Scenario
3. List what you can reasonably do to alter the outcome: Your Action Plan

Conclude by spending five minutes breathing and releasing all thoughts, all worries, and all fretting in regards to the matter. Picture a positive outcome and ask your brilliant brain to spend its night connecting all the dots you will need to create a successful outcome. Put a good night's sleep at the top of your action plan, hit the sheets, and make it a habit to use this same tactic for all stress-induced fretting and brooding.

Soon, your brain will begin formulating those lists long before you've reached the fretting and brooding stage, which will help you relinquish the unnecessary fretting and brooding, thereby reducing your stress, improving your sleep, and nourishing your brain. This is a strategy that can help you address virtually any financial issue—while you sleep!

GOOD DREAMS, GOOD FORTUNE

Remember, sleep is as good for your bank balance as it is for your brain because it:

- Is essential to your overall health and well-being.
- Gives your body—and your brain—time to restore, repair, and regenerate.
- Elevates your moods and gives you more energy.
- Makes it easier to handle normal life stressors.
- Helps your brain learn, grow, and master new skills.

Train your brain to get a good night's sleep and you'll be at the top of your game. It's that simple. Sweet dreams!

CHAPTER 13

EAT YOUR WAY TO WEALTH

Principle: Your brain is a bodily organ dependent upon you to supply the nutrients it needs to be able to function at peak capacity.

If you want your brain to work at its peak capacity—as well as continue to grow—it's absolutely vital that you nourish it well. Consider this: Your brain constitutes about 2 percent of your total body weight, yet it uses 20 percent of your body's blood supply. It also uses 20 percent of your body's total oxygen supply and 65 percent of its glucose. Those numbers mean your brain requires a host of nutrients in order to remain healthy and function at its peak capacity.

FEED YOUR BRAIN

Before we discuss your brain's specific nutritional needs, here's a quick quiz to assess your eating habits. Are you feeding your brain what it needs to be the best it can be?

1. **You eat according to the USDA's MyPlate guidelines at:**
   A. every meal
   B. most meals
   C. only by accident
   D. What's MyPlate?

2. **You eat fast food:**
   A. never
   B. occasionally
   C. once or twice a week
   D. supersize me!

3. **For breakfast, you eat:**
   A. oatmeal, low-fat milk, and fruit
   B. bacon and eggs
   C. coffee and doughnuts
   D. What's breakfast?

4. **When it comes to fats:**
   A. omega-3 fatty acids are your only source of fats
   B. you limit yourself to "good" fats
   C. trans fats never pass your lips
   D. What's a trans fat?

5. **Your major sources of protein is/are:**
   A. low-fat dairy, fish, and legumes
   B. chicken and fish
   C. meat
   D. spam

6. You drink alcohol:

    A. occasionally

    B. a glass of red wine once a day

    C. more than twice a day

    D. Why drink when you can do drugs?

Answer Key

If you checked mostly As, you understand that you have to feed your brain well for it to perform well. But if you want the sharpest, most creative brain in town, there's always more you can do to keep your brain healthy and humming along.

If you checked mostly Bs, you are at least paying attention to what you eat, but there's a lot you can do to feed your little gray cells with better fuel. Improving your nutrition will facilitate the increased creativity, drive, focus, and neuronal growth that will take you to the next level.

If you checked mostly Cs, your lackadaisical attitude toward nutrition is costing you brainpower—power that you need to promote good brain health and become the successful person you long to be. Feed your brain well, and you may see instant results in your pocketbook.

If you checked mostly Ds, you are thwarting your brain health with every bite. You need to adjust your eating and drinking habits dramatically if you expect your brain to help you on your quest for wealth—and health. Your brain is crying out for the nourishment it needs to function and flourish.

It doesn't take a neuroscientist to deduce that what you eat plays a vital role in how well your brain functions and how it continues to grow. In fact, the food choices you consume affect virtually every cell, organ, and system in your body. A healthful diet provides your cells with everything they need to function well, reproduce, and repair damage. Unhealthy food choices not only make every cell work harder, they can outright damage your body—and your brain.

> ### Your Brain Comes First
>
> One of the easiest ways to recognize nutrition deficiency is not from a change in body activity but from a change in mental functioning. This is because the frontal lobes, the area of the brain that acts like the CEO of you, are particularly sensitive to falling glucose levels, while brain areas regulating vital functions like breathing, heartbeat, and liver function are more hardy. Researchers at Roehampton University in England noted that, "When your glucose level drops, the symptom is confused thinking, not a change in breathing pattern." Another early sign of a glucose drop is a change in mood, irritability, and overall grumpiness. Keeping your brain well fed keeps it functioning well!

THE BOTTOM LINE OF FOOD CHOICES

The more you know about nutrition, the better, but you don't have to be smarter than a third-grader to understand and incorporate the following extremely basic principle: Some foods are very good for your body (and your brain); other foods, not so much.

Foods That Improve Your Health (and Wealth):

- Colorful fruits and vegetables that are rich in antioxidants and fiber
- High-fiber, whole-grain foods (brown rice, whole-wheat bread, whole-wheat pasta, and oats)

- Protein (fish, poultry, soy, lean meats, legumes, eggs, low-fat dairy, nuts, and seeds); omega-3 fatty acids found in fish, flax-seed oil, and some nuts
- Nutrient-dense foods (foods in their leanest or lowest-fat forms and without added fats, sugars, starches, or sodium)

Foods That Adversely Affect Your Health (and Wealth):

- Excess saturated fat (fatty red meat, cheese, ice cream, and fried food)
- Trans fat (margarines, donuts, pies, cakes, cookies, chips, and fast food)
- Refined carbohydrates (white rice, white bread, and pasta)
- High-calorie food (containing an excess of solid fats and added sugars)
- Processed foods (containing an excess of solid fats and added sugars)
- Foods with high sodium content
- Beverages with high sugar content (sodas, in particular)

The United States Department of Agriculture (USDA) reports that Americans typically have 35 percent of their total calories consumed as solid fats and added sugars, on average, in contrast to a recommended limit of no more than about 5 to 15 percent of total calories for most individuals.

THE USDA'S BOTTOM LINE ON FOOD CHOICES

The USDA consistently researches nutrition and provides a food guide, called MyPlate, to help Americans make the healthiest food choices. The plate conveys three messages when it comes to choosing food that will meet your nutritional requirements: variety, balance, and moderation. The amount of food you need from each food group depends on your age, sex, and level of physical activity. We've provided general guidelines below, but you can find more information at *www.MyPlate.gov.*

The food groups in the plate include the following:

- **Whole-grain breads, cereal, rice, and pasta (complex carbohydrates):** roughly 25–30 percent of your plate, and for adults 6–8 ounces of grains per day. Half of your daily grains should be whole grains.
- **Fresh vegetables:** Roughly 30 percent of your plate. Healthy adult men and women should eat 2–3 cups of vegetables per day, and vegetables should be varied among vegetable subgroups (such as dark leafy greens, starchy vegetables, and red and orange vegetables).
- **Fresh fruits:** Roughly 20 percent of your plate. Note that, added with vegetables, 50 percent of your plate at every meal should be made from fruits and vegetables. Healthy adults should eat 1.5–2 cups of fruits per day.
- **Low-fat or nonfat milk, yogurt, and cheese:** Shown as a glass to the side of your plate. Healthy adults should have three cups of calcium-rich dairy products per day. Importantly, foods made from milk that have little to no calcium, such as cream cheese, cream, and butter, are not part of the dairy group.
- **Lean meat, poultry, fish, dry beans, eggs, nuts, and meat substitutes:** Roughly 20 percent of your plate. Healthy adults should eat 5–6 ounce. of lean protein daily, and the USDA recommends that at least 8 ounces per week should come from lean seafood sources.

Sweets and fats are not part of MyPlate, and thus should be used very sparingly.

How Much Is Too Much?

Most people overestimate serving sizes, particularly with the distortions caused by super-sized restaurant meals. Ideally, servings are as follows:

- **One serving of whole grains:** 1 slice of bread; l ounce of ready-to-eat cereal; ½ cup of cooked whole-grain cereal, rice, or pasta
- **One serving of vegetables:** 1 cup of raw leafy vegetables; ½ cup of other vegetables, cooked or chopped raw; ¾ cup of vegetable juice
- **One serving of fruit:** 1 medium apple, banana, or orange; ½ cup of chopped, cooked, or canned fruit; ¾ cup fruit juice
- **One serving of dairy:** 1 cup of milk or yogurt; 1½ ounces of natural cheese; 2 ounces of processed cheese
- **One serving of protein sources:** 3–4 ounces of cooked lean meat, poultry, or fish; ½ cup of cooked dry beans; 2 tablespoons of peanut butter; ⅓ cup of nuts; or 1 egg

Holy Pathogen Batman!

According to a recent study published in the journal *Cell*, our brains may react to excess food as if it were a pathogen. The resulting immune response, which occurs irrespective of weight gain, may cause cognitive deficits such as those associated with Alzheimer's. Similarly, high blood sugar, coupled with a cognitive task, has been associated with elevated cortisol, the hormone known to impair memory in high doses. Rats that gorged on saturated fat for several weeks had obvious damage to the hippocampus—a brain area critical to memory formation.

Budget Your Calories!

The amount of calories you can eat without adding weight depends on your age, gender, and your level of physical activity, and it declines as you get older. To find out your ideal calorie intake, consult with your doctor. In the meantime, consider these as rough guidelines:

Adult women who are sedentary or only mildly active: 1,600 calories per day. Physically active women can add another 600 or so calories. Pregnant women can add even more.

Adult men who are sedentary or only mildly active: 2,200 calories per day. Physically active men can add 600 calories.

CELLULAR SUICIDE

Researchers at the Salk Institute in California found that sugar damages cells everywhere in the body, especially brain cells. Furthermore, researchers at the University of Wisconsin found that the brain may react to excess refined sugars as if they were a virus or bacteria, creating an immune response that can lead to cognitive deficits such as those associated with Alzheimer's disease. Similarly, high blood sugar coupled with performing a mentally challenging task is associated with high levels of cortisol, which impairs memory. In other words, that dessert you ate at lunch might stress out you, your body, and your brain . . . and affect your afternoon work efficiency!

Excessive refined sugar can:

- Block membranes and thereby slow down your neural communication.
- Increase free radical inflammatory stress on your brain. Free radicals can rupture cells.
- Interfere with synaptic communication.
- Cause neurons to misfire and send erroneous messages that take time and energy to sort out.

- Increase delta, alpha, and theta brain waves. These are slower brain waves, which can make it harder to think clearly.
- Eventually damage your neurons.

Permanently Cross Soda Off Your List

Your brain uses 65 percent of your body's glucose, but too much or too little glucose can have a detrimental effect on brain function. One can of soda contains 10 teaspoons of table sugar, all of which floods into a bloodstream that typically contains a total of 4 teaspoons of blood sugar. The rush alerts your pancreas to release a lot of insulin. Some sugar is quickly ushered into the cells, including brain cells, and the rest goes into storage or into fat cells. An hour later, your blood sugar may fall dramatically, creating low blood sugar, and these rapid swings produce symptoms of impaired memory and clouded thinking.

Why Diet Soda Is Also Off the Table

Stroke is the third leading cause of death, behind heart disease and cancer, and recent research uncovered a possible link between drinking diet soda and suffering a stroke. Previous research had revealed that those who drank more than one soft drink a day, whether regular or diet, were more likely than nondrinkers to have metabolic syndrome, a cluster of risk factors including high blood pressure, elevated triglycerides, low levels of good cholesterol, high fasting blood sugar, and large waists.

When Hannah Gardener, an epidemiologist at the University of Miami Miller School of Medicine, studied approximately 2,500 people (average age of sixty-nine) over a period of nine years, she found that those who drank diet soda daily, compared to those who drank no soda, were 61 percent more likely to suffer a stroke. During what is known as the Northern Manhattan Study, Gardener controlled for such factors as age, gender, ethnicity, physical activity, calorie intake, smoking, and alcohol drinking habits. After controlling for the presence of metabolic syndrome, vascular disease in the limbs, and a history of heart disease, Gardener reviewed her results again, and found the link was closer 48 percent, which still poses a significant risk level.

Some fellow researchers noted that the study found a possible association between diet soda and stroke risk, without clearly demonstrating a cause and effect. Still, these dubious researchers also noted that Gardener's results warranted more rigorous testing.

WHAT ABOUT SALT?

Although most research has been conducted in adults, the adverse effects of sodium on blood pressure begin early in life, and there is gathering evidence that salt intake can increase the risk of stroke. In a separate study from the one mentioned above, Hannah Gardener also found high salt intake was linked to a higher risk of stroke. Using the same data gathered in her study of diet soda, she evaluated the salt intake of the approximately 2,500 participants over a period of nearly ten years. During that time, those who consumed more than 4,000 milligrams a day of sodium had more than double the risk of ischemic stroke than those who consumed less than 1,500 milligrams a day.

A Gathering of Bs

Vitamin B could very well stand for "Vitamin Brain." The B vitamins (1, 2, 3, 6, and 12) all offer individual support to your brain, but when you take them in conjunction with one another, you can boost their individual benefits to the highest level. Bs are vital because they help maintain healthy brain cells, metabolize the carbohydrates used as fuel to your brain, produce neurotransmitters, and improve your moods. People lacking in essential B vitamins have shown an increased risk for depression, anxiety, memory loss, irritability, confusion, abnormal brain waves, and Alzheimer's disease.

How much salt is too much? The U.S. Dietary Guidelines for Americans were recently adjusted downward to no more than 1,500 milligrams a day. The best way to combat excessive salt intake is to limit processed foods, and high-salt foods such as cured meats, luncheon meats, many cheeses, most canned soups and vegetables, boxed rice with "seasoning," and soy sauce. Always check the sodium content per serving, and if you eat processed foods, choose those that are lower in salt.

Your Mother Was Right: Eat More Fruits and Vegetables

When oxygen cells go rogue, they form free radicals that can damage your body in a multitude of ways. Free radical oxygen builds up in your brain faster than anywhere else in your body, which damages brain cells, creating a sort of biological rust. Luckily, dark green spinach, broccoli rabe, pumpkin, pomegranates, raspberries, yellow peppers, and other high-intensity, brightly colored fruits and vegetables are packed with highly desirable phytochemicals, while dark-green, red, and purple foods, like spinach, blueberries, eggplants, and purple cabbage, contain antioxidants. Together, they cut those free radicals off at the pass, as well as turn on the genes that boost your body's natural antioxidant system. Thanks, Mom!

SUPERACHIEVERS START THEIR DAY WITH A BANG

After a good night's rest, your body—and your brain—need to replenish their blood sugar stores, which are your body's main source of energy. Your brain in particular needs a fresh supply of glucose each day (because it doesn't store glucose). Breakfast eaters tend to experience better concentration, problem-solving ability, strength, and endurance.

Don't know what to eat? Try these suggestions:

- Dry, vitamin-fortified cereal with sliced fruit and skim milk
- Low-fat or nonfat yogurt with fruit or low-fat granola cereal
- Peanut butter on a whole-wheat bagel and orange juice
- A small bran muffin, a banana, and low-fat or skim milk
- Oatmeal with raisins or berries or walnuts (or all three!)
- A breakfast smoothie (blended fruit and skim milk)
- A hard-boiled egg, half a grapefruit, and a slice of whole-grain bread
- Cottage cheese and peaches

GOOD FAT, GREAT CELLS

Fats are vital to a healthy diet. Fats help carry, absorb, and store the fat-soluble vitamins (A, D, E, and K) in your bloodstream. Approximately 60 percent of your brain matter consists of fats that create *all* the cell membranes in the body. However, some fats are good, and some are bad. If your diet is loaded with bad fats, your brain can only make low-quality nerve cell membranes that don't function well; if your diet provides the essential, good fats, your brain cells can manufacture higher-quality nerve cell membranes and influence positively your nerve cells' ability to function at their peak capacity. Unfortunately, even good fats are a very concentrated source of energy, providing more than double the amount of calories in one gram of carbohydrate or protein, which is why it's key to choose the healthy fats and to eat them in moderation.

The good fats, or lipids, that are necessary for your body—and your brain—to function optimally are called *fatty acids*. Essential fatty acids cannot be manufactured in your body, so you have to eat them (or take supplements). Your body uses fatty acids to produce hormone-like substances that regulate a wide range of functions, including blood pressure, blood clotting, blood lipid levels, the immune response, and the inflammation response to injury or infection.

Eat What Bill Clinton Eats Now

When former President Bill Clinton, a man who loved greasy hamburgers and fried foods, adopted a plant-based, near-vegan diet, he lost twenty-four pounds within months, reaching a weight he hadn't seen since his teens. Reportedly, Clinton got on board after reviewing extensive scientific data that a plant-based diet could not only stem but could actually reverse arterial blockage. Most notably, in a study dating back to 1987, Dr. Dean Ornish found that 82 percent of his study participants (more than 200 people) who adopted a plant-based diet, along with moderate walking, yoga, and social support, decreased their arterial blockage within one year. Bill Clinton has essentially become a poster child for plant-based diets, and it's obvious that his brain continues to function at peak capacity.

Rock Those Omega-3s

Omega-3 fatty acids should be at the top of your shopping list. However, they are fats, so you want to get the maximum benefit while consuming the fewest calories. Some foods containing omega-3 fatty acids are especially good for your brain, such as:

- Certain cold-water fish (bluefish, herring, mackerel, rainbow trout, salmon, sardines, tuna, and whitefish)
- Olive oil
- Flaxseed oil
- Peanut oil
- Canola oil

Omega-3 fatty acids are great for mental clarity, concentration, and focus. In fact, omega-3 fatty acids seem to be particularly important for brain health in children and adolescents. In 2010, a multinational research group found that omega-3 fatty acids may help to prevent psychiatric disorders in children. Somewhat alarmingly, the typical American child has a diet containing little omega-3 fatty acids. Purdue researchers have linked this absence of good fats to a higher risk of attention deficit disorder and other learning disabilities.

Pick Up the Flax

If you need to sharpen your focus, try taking one tablespoon of ground flaxseed daily. It's an excellent source of alpha-linolenic acid (ALA), a healthy fat that improves the workings of the cerebral cortex, the area of the brain that processes sensory information, including that of pleasure. To meet your daily quota, sprinkle it on salads or mix it into a smoothie or shake.

Bad Fats, Bloated Brain

Essential fatty acids are the most important nutrients for your brain, but most American diets fall short on these good essential fats and include way too many saturated, hydrogenated, and partially hydrogenated trans fats. Bad fats (saturated and processed fats) are the ones that remain solid when refrigerated, and are typically found in:

- Commercial baked goods such as pies, cakes, doughnuts, and cookies.
- Processed foods, such as crackers, potato chips, corn chips, cheese puffs, pretzels, and candy

- Fast foods
- Fatty cuts of beef, pork, and lamb
- Dairy products like butter (and margarines), whole milk, ice cream, and cheese
- Mayonnaise and some salad dressings
- Palm, palm kernel, and coconut oils

In contrast to healthy fatty acids (whose soft pliability helps nerve cell membranes function smoothly), these trans fatty acids (called "partially hydrogenated oils" on food packaging) become double bonded, rigid, and thus tend to gum up synaptic or electrical nerve cell communication. Besides greatly increasing your chance of gaining too much weight on foods that contain little to zero nutritional value, trans fats:

- Alter the synthesis of neurotransmitters, such as dopamine.
- Increase LDL (bad) cholesterol and decrease HDL (good) cholesterol.
- Increase the amount of plaque in blood vessels and increase the possibility of blood clots forming, both of which put your heart—and your brain—at risk.
- Disrupt the production of energy in the mitochondria (the energy factories) of brain cells.
- Increase the amount of triglycerides in your system, which slows down the amount of oxygen going to your brain, and the excess of which has been linked to depression.

One reason America has become a nation of overweight people is that our consumption of essential fatty acids has declined by more than 80 percent while our consumption of trans fats has skyrocketed more than 2,500 percent!

Facing a Mental Challenge?

If you are, B vitamins, such as folic acid, B12, and B6 help facilitate messages being sent back and forth throughout your brain and your body. If you've got a mental challenge ahead, eating a small portion of seafood, leafy dark-green vegetables, or a cup of cranberries will help you stay focused and more alert. A bowl of whole-grain cereal, juice, and a sliced egg will also get your mental motor running. Or whip up a smoothie using fruits such as pears, apples, and berries mixed with whey protein and kelp powder. Bananas, nuts, and seeds are also excellent foods to eat when you need a burst of brainpower. Remember to keep sugar consumption low as it tends to spike your blood sugar levels, and don't eat too much or your body will be focused on digestion when you want it focused on performance.

NOT QUITE THE WAKE-UP DRUG YOU THINK IT IS

Downing those cups of coffee in the morning may fire up your neurons, but studies show that caffeine only increases the output and quality of your work if the work you're doing doesn't require nuance or abstract thinking. Caffeine seems to speed your thinking processes up a bit, and improve memory creation and retention when it comes to declarative memory, the kind you use when memorizing lists. It doesn't seem to help at all when it comes to creative energy, or thinking beyond the basics. Thanks to the increasing tolerance that comes with regular consumption, it eventually takes more and more caffeine to get the same effect.

It's also true that consuming too much caffeine can irritate your stomach, cause headaches, create anxiety, serve as a diuretic, and disturb your sleep. And it's important to note that caffeine is not only found in coffee beans but also in tea leaves, cocoa beans, and products derived from these sources. You may not be aware that caffeine is also found in more than a thousand different over-the-counter and prescription drugs and that there is a very small amount of caffeine in decaffeinated coffee.

Caffeine Budget

As long as you still drink plenty of healthy beverages, such as water, fruit juice, milk, or green tea, you can have a few cups of coffee and feel perfectly good about it. The pharmacological active dose of caffeine is defined as 200 milligrams, and the daily recommended not-to-exceed intake level is the equivalent of one to three cups of coffee per day (139 to 417 milligrams). Below is a guideline for approximate amounts of caffeine in commonly used foods and beverages:

- Coffee, brewed from ground beans: 6 ounces = 100 milligrams
- Tea, brewed from whole leaves: 6 ounces = 10–50 milligrams
- Cola, can or bottle: 12 ounces = 50 milligrams
- Cocoa, as milk chocolate bar: 1 ounce = 6 milligrams
- Semisweet chocolate chips: 1 cup = 92 milligrams

Don't Toss Out the Coffee Quite Yet

Our brains have a thin coating that separates it from the rest of the body called the "blood-brain barrier." This vital coating can become susceptible to damage from disease and stress, and researchers have recently found some evidence that the caffeine in coffee products may actually help to protect the coating and repair the damage, as well as ward off other harmful invaders. So score one for the cup of java—just don't take this news as permission to drink too much caffeine every day!

FOOD FOR OVERACHIEVERS

Some foods are called superfoods because they offer extraordinary improvements for your body by providing essential nutrients. A healthy diet that contains a variety of superfoods helps you maintain your weight, fight disease, live longer, and function at your peak capacity. And when your brain is functioning at its peak capacity, it'll be easier for you to train it to get rich!

Fish for Wealth

Fish is loaded with omega-3 fatty acids, as well as protein, vitamins, and minerals, and is particularly good for your brain. A study of 2,000 Norwegians, aged seventy to seventy-four, found that those who ate fish of any kind were two to three times less likely to perform poorly on cognitive tests.

Go Wild for Salmon

Salmon is one of the best fish you can eat for your brain. However, farm-raised salmon is often injected with antibiotics and often contains 70 percent more fat than wild salmon, and 200 percent more fat than wild Pacific pink salmon and chum salmon. Wild salmon is drug free and also has higher levels of the beneficial omega-3 fatty acids. So go wild when it comes to salmon, and your brain will love you for it!

The USDA and the American Heart Association recommend eating two eight-ounce servings of fish per week, but caution against eating too much seafood, particularly if it has a higher level of mercury content. For seafood that is higher in mercury content—shark, swordfish, king mackerel, tilefish, canned albacore (white) tuna, tuna steaks, lobster, halibut, and orange roughy—they caution against eating more than one six-ounce serving, which is about the size of two decks of cards or two checkbooks.

Seafood lower in mercury include shrimp, canned light tuna (not albacore tuna), salmon, pollock, catfish, cod, crab, flounder/sole, grouper, haddock, herring, mahi-mahi, ocean perch, oysters, rainbow trout, sardines, scallops, spiny lobster, tilapia, and trout.

Bank on Berries

When it comes to brain protection, there's nothing quite like blueberries. Among its treasures are antioxidant and anti-inflammatory compounds, which some studies indicate may offer potential for reversing short-term memory loss and forestalling many other effects of aging. In a study on reversing memory loss reported in the *Wall Street Journal*, blueberries had the strongest impact on the mental function of aging rodents than any of the other fruits tested.

Plus, blueberries have 38 percent more antioxidants than red wine. One cup of blueberries reportedly provides three to five times the antioxidants as five servings of carrots, broccoli, squash, and apples. What this means for your health is a lower risk of heart disease; vibrant, firm skin; and a boost in brainpower. Eat them spring, summer, winter, and fall. Eat them frozen in smoothies or mixed with yogurt and walnuts as a real brain pleaser. If you can swing it, eat ½ cup of blueberries every day.

Berries are so nutritious and good for the brain because their colorful skins contain flavonoids, which have been shown to have antioxidant abilities. Flavonoids are also found in green tea, soy, apples, and cherries, but they are most potent in red and purple fruits. Other berries that are potent antioxidants for your brain are acai berries, goji berries, mulberries, boysenberries, and cranberries. The fruits with the highest capacity to absorb free radicals are (in order of potency): blueberries, blackberries, strawberries, raspberries, and plums.

Opt for Lower Glycemic Carbohydrates

Your frontal cortex (your brain's CEO) requires a steady stream of glucose to function well. Glucose primarily comes from carbohydrates, which are ranked according to how quickly your body breaks down and absorbs their glucose molecules (the "glycemic scale"). The faster they break down, the higher they measure on the scale. And in this case, you don't want a perfect ten. Some higher glycemic carbohydrates, like pretzels or donuts, are broken down very quickly, causing your blood sugar to spike, and then rather quickly drop. Raw vegetables, like carrots or broccoli, are lower on the index and thus provide a slower, steadier stream of energy to your brain—and keep you feeling full longer. To best serve your brain, choose high-fiber carbohydrates and combine them with healthy fats or protein to slow absorption even more. Beans are a great resource for a steady stream of glucose. Whatever you choose, you don't need a lot. Your brain works best with about 25 grams of glucose circulating in your bloodstream, about the amount found in a banana. To optimize brainpower, eat more frequent but smaller meals.

Booster Shot

When it comes to boosting brainpower, Dr. Andrew Scholey, a researcher at the University of Northumbria in England, reported powerful results when combining gingko biloba and ginseng. A dose of 400 milligrams of ginseng reflected immediate improvements in memory (storage, holding, and retrieval), whereas a dose of 360 milligrams of ginkgo reflected faster mental reaction times. Combining the doses to reach 960 milligrams (60 percent ginseng and 40 percent gingko) revved up available mental energy. Subjects in the study were able to subtract the number seven repeatedly from a variety of figures, just as rapidly as they could subtract threes (considered much easier). Both supplements are believed to increase oxygen levels in your brain.

Choose Nuts for a Smacking Good Bonus

Nuts are high in fat but also supply the good fats, as well as minerals, fiber, and protein. Walnuts, almonds, hazelnuts, and pecans all pack healthy fats that help keep your arteries clear, helping blood and oxygen flow freely to your brain. Major bonus: Nuts also provide the raw materials your body uses to produce mood-boosting serotonin in your brain, and they also contain magnesium, which helps to insulate your nerve fibers to help them fire faster and with more efficiency. Thus, you will get better-working, happier neurons!

All nuts are high in calories from fat, so limit your intake to one ounce or about twelve walnut halves or twenty-four almonds, ideally spread throughout the day for little protein and fat pick-me-ups.

Fire White Rice, Hire Quinoa

Once known as "the gold of the Incas," this hearty little grain-like crop has more protein, iron, and unsaturated fats and fewer carbohydrates than any real grain on the market. A complete protein, quinoa provides ten essential amino acids and is packed with minerals, B vitamins, and fiber. It also contains high amounts of the amino acid lysine, which is essential for tissue growth and repair. It's a great source of manganese as well as magnesium, iron, copper, phosphorus, and the B vitamins, especially folate, another essential nutrient needed for the formation and development of new and normal body tissue. (Your body cannot make folate, so it must be obtained from foods and supplements.)

Sweep Out Your Arteries with Oats

Oats are a marvelous source of energy, and oat bran is an excellent fiber that can reduce serum cholesterol. Whether you choose steel-cut oats (the most roughly cut and least processed), rolled or "old-fashioned" oats, quick oats, or instant, all types of oats are effective at reducing cholesterol—as long as you eat 2 ounces of oat bran (⅔ cup dry or about 1½ cups cooked) or 3 ounces of oatmeal

(1 cup dry or 2 cups cooked). As an alternative, sprinkle oat bran on cereal and yogurt, or add it to toppings for fruit crisps and casseroles. You an also use oat bran to coat chicken, lean meats, or fish before baking, or add it to meat loaf or meatballs in place of some of the breadcrumbs.

A Triple Bonus

Three superfoods that will make you mentally sharp are:

- **Lentils:** They provide a steady stream of lower glycemic glucose, which can improve your brain's ability to come up with new ideas and thoughts.
- **Chia seeds:** They're a great source of omega-3 fatty acids, have more antioxidants than blueberries, and improve brain cell communication.
- **Brazil nuts:** They're loaded with (healthy) monounsaturated fat, which helps your brain communicate with your body. They also provide riboflavin, or B2, which is necessary for the proper production of cellular energy in your body. Plus, they have high amounts of potassium and magnesium, which helps lower your blood pressure and strengthen your heart.

Soy Good, Soy Flexible

Soy protein appears to lower blood cholesterol levels, decreasing blood clots and platelet clumping, both of which can increase the risk for a heart attack or stroke. Soy also improves the elasticity of arteries, which makes blood flow better, and reduces oxidation of low-density lipoprotein (LDL or "bad" cholesterol), which can lower the risk of plaque formation. Soy can be found in edamame (green soy beans), mature soy beans, soy nuts, soy milk, tofu (coagulated soy), tempeh (fermented soybean cake), soy sauce, and miso (fermented soy). There are also soy-based cheeses and dairy products, as well as soy bean oil.

Minimize Liabilities

Some foods are known to interfere with healthy brain functioning. Specifically, you should limit alcohol, sugar, aspartame sweetener, and MSG (monosodium glutamate). Alcohol makes you dull; sugar makes you foggy; aspartame and MSG can kill brain cells. Also avoid processed foods that are loaded with sugar, additives, or stimulants, as they tend to worsen depression symptoms. Severely limit artificial food colorings, corn syrup, icing, and white bread. Instead, stick to foods that are good for your brain and make you smarter as a bonus.

Adding just one serving a day of soy can make a difference. Note: If you have a family member who has had breast cancer, check with your doctor before adding a lot of soy to your diet.

WELCOME CHOCOLATE TO YOUR BOARDROOM

Yes, it's true, chocolate is good for body and brain—in moderation. In a study done by Salk Institute researcher Henriette van Praag and colleagues, a compound found in cocoa, epicatechin, combined with exercise, was found to promote functional changes in a part of the brain involved in the formation of learning and memory. Choose dark, semisweet chocolate for the best nutritional value. Milk chocolate has too much saturated fat and sugar. Instead, opt for organic or fair-trade dark chocolate (cacao beans should be listed as an ingredient) with 70 percent, or more, cocoa. If the chocolate has been sweetened with raw organic sugar cane or honey, that's preferable to other sugars. Your ideal chocolate budget: two or three small squares, no more than three times a week.

The Great Dilator

If you have high blood pressure and you love dark chocolate, you're in luck. In fifteen recent studies, researchers discovered that dark chocolate significantly reduced blood pressure—with one caveat, as long as the person already had high blood pressure. Those with normal to low blood pressure don't experience the same benefit. It's believed that flavonoids found in dark chocolate cause blood vessels to dilate, which can lower high blood pressure as much as thirty minutes of exercise would do and may reduce the risk of heart attack by as much as 20 percent over five years. Also good news: Half an ounce or about one small square of dark chocolate will do the trick!

Chocolate Assets

Your brain loves chocolate because it:

- contains serotonin, which makes your brain happy.
- contains a neurotransmitter that provides a natural high and calms your neurological system, reducing anxiety.
- contains flavonoids (plant pigments) that are responsible for antioxidant activity and help protect your good cholesterol and arterial linings, as well as inhibit an enzyme that causes inflammation.
- contains an amino acid that helps your blood vessels dilate, serving as a natural anti-inflammatory, regulating blood pressure and blood flow.
- contains phytochemicals, which increase your body's ability to block arterial damage caused by free radicals and inhibit platelet aggregation, which could cause a heart attack or stroke.

All that, and it also contains theobromine, caffeine, and other substances that can improve concentration and focus. Bring on the dark chocolate!

Chocolate Trumps Red Wine!

According to study results published in the American Chemical Society's *Journal of Agriculture and Food Chemistry,* cocoa powder has nearly twice the antioxidants of red wine and up to three times that found in green tea. In fact, dark chocolate tested higher for antioxidants than fruits and vegetables. Its closest competitor, milk chocolate, came in second, and prunes came in third.

Everyone's Brain Is Different

Despite broad similarities, food affects everyone's brain a little differently. For whatever reason, extroverts are more likely to succumb to a post-lunch dip, an intense desire to nap, or to chug coffee mid-afternoon. Children and the very thin may feel faint or grumpy, due to low blood glucose, faster than an average-sized adult. A minor dip in glucose may make people who chronically undereat, overexercise, or regularly skip meals feel fuzzyheaded. Their brains have essentially become sensitized to not getting enough. So listen to our advice—but listen to your own body, too, and do what seems to make sense to you . . . and your brain.

OPTIMAL HEALTH, OPTIMAL BRAIN

Hundreds of macro- and micronutrients that could directly and indirectly affect your brain health are being touted in books and on websites, but we always recommend talking with your doctor before adding supplements or herbs. It's also wise to seek out information about the latest science, as new brain discoveries are happening weekly, if not daily. Just remember that a supersmart person doesn't try untested fads or take any supplements without fully researching side effects, which also means determining how anything added will affect medications already being taken.

In general, if you eat a healthy diet and bolster it with super-foods, you and your brain should enjoy optimal health and perform at optimal levels. Whatever you do, remember that your brain may not be visible to your naked eye, but it plays a vital role in every aspect of your life. Nurture it well, and it will definitely reward you—financially as well as in every other aspect of your life.

SPECIFIC THINGS YOU CAN DO TO TRAIN YOUR BRAIN TO GET RICH

Throughout the book, we've offered specific techniques for nourishing, protecting, and optimizing your brainpower. We are fully aware that a lot of the material was science heavy and required an effort to digest—which is also, by the way, very good for your brain. Therefore, we wanted to close with a list of specific actions you can take, within the context of the techniques we've discussed, that will train your brain to get rich. After reviewing the book, you may be able to create your own list, even more specific to your circumstances.

1. Know yourself and identify the values that inspire you to become the best you can be.

2. Determine what being rich really means to you, identify ways to achieve it, and plot your quest for success.

3. Familiarize yourself with the latest neuroscience and neurobiology, and then adopt techniques that will bolster your brainpower.

4. Identify your individual brain's strengths and weaknesses and take action to make it a finely tuned thinking machine.

5. Know which activities energize and motivate your brain—and which activities put your brain to sleep or, even worse, damage it.

6. Avoid toxic environments, whether it's the people you hang out with or your workplace.

7. Surround yourself with optimistic, creative thinkers whose very presence lights up your mirror neurons.

8. Strengthen your left PFC so you will feel happier in your job—and feel more sensitive and compassionate towards your employees and your customers.

9. Take an active role in setting clear intentions and goals to enlist your brain's assistance in manifesting your desires.

10. Improve your brain's ability to focus on the most important tasks.

11. Be willing to invest the time and energy required to fully engage your brain and make it your ally.

12. Improve your ability to remember past successes so your brain will help you recreate them (rather than fall sway to fear by focusing on past failures).

13. Employ imagination and visualization to create a mental picture that your brain will perceive as already true and thereby lead you down the neuronal path to successful re-creation.

14. Improve memory retention and your ability to process and integrate new information.

15. Develop your intuitive abilities.

16. Do things to shake up the way you traditionally think.

17. Do something that requires you to use the parts of your brain that don't get enough stimulation.

18. Avoid black-and-white thinking; embrace nuance.

19. Flip the way you view or think about things. Instead of why, ask why not?

20. Challenge your brain to strengthen existing neuronal pathways and generate new ones.

21. Expand your knowledge to keep your brain primed to learn new skills.

22. Choose activities that create positive rewards and increase your serotonin levels.

23. Purposefully reinforce with positive rewards, in healthy doses and ways (nonaddictive).

24. Tamp down an overactive amygdala to quiet irrational fears and to make it easier for your brain to process and integrate information and improve decision-making.

25. Decrease stress levels so your brain is not being overtaxed or drowning in cortisol.

26. Take calculated risks to keep your brain flexible and eager to explore new opportunities.

27. Use meditation to teach your brain how to pare down distractions and focus on what needs to be done.

28. Train your brain to drown out negative thoughts and respond more readily to positive thoughts.

29. Make creativity a habit so your brain knows exactly what to do when you call upon it for solutions and innovation.

30. Nourish your body so you can reap the rewards of a fully functioning brain and display success that will inspire those around you.

31. Keep the bloodlines open and flexible so your brain continues to function and grow.

32. Give your brain breathing space and restorative play to keep it refreshed and ready to fire neurons when you need them most.

INDEX

A

Acetylcholine, 32
Addictive tendencies, 32, 130–31
Ali, Muhammad, 155–56
Allen, Dr. Karen, 200
Allman, John, 59
Alpha waves, 50–51, 174
Altman, Dr. Joseph, 42
Alzheimer's disease, 26, 161, 197, 199, 227–28, 230
Amygdala, 29–30, 55, 124–25
Anterior cingulate cortex (ACC), 28–29, 55–59
Anticipation, 58, 183, 188
Assumptions, making, 66–69
Atrophy, 198
Automatic responses, 65–66
Automatic thoughts, 61–66, 69
Axons, 20–21

B

Basal ganglia, 30–31, 126
Bayer, Dr. Shirley, 42
Behavior gap, 129
"Being rich." *See also* "Being wealthy"
   being happy and, 9, 12–13
   belief in, 61–82
   intentions of, 83–104
   meaning of, 6–7
   meditation and, 165–77
   training for, 105–33

working at, 135–64
"Being wealthy." *See also* "Being rich"
   characteristics for, 11–12
   exercise for, 195–202
   explanation of, 1–16
   happiness and, 12–13
   meaning of, 8–12
   nutrition for, 221–46
   paying attention to, 89–91
   playful activities for, 179–94
   sleep requirements for, 203–19
   specific brain areas for, 54–60
Beta waves, 50–51
Boredom, 151, 154
Brain
   age-proofing, 198
   areas of, 21–31
   capabilities of, 6, 211
   cortex, 22–27
   deep brain structures, 28–29
   feeding, 221–22
   goal setting and, 101–8
   improving function of, 159–61
   insightful brain, 111–14, 135–39
   instinctual brain, 110–14, 117–18, 135
   laziness of, 82, 135, 151
   limitations of, 6, 64–65, 126
   molding, 14, 36–39, 151
   motivating, 7–8, 90, 95, 201–2
   new studies of, 39–46
   optimal brain, 245–46

D

Davidson, Richard, 45, 87

Decision-making, 40–41, 123, 140–44. *See also* Financial decisions

Delta waves, 51–52

Dementia, 161

Dendrites, 20

Destiny, 13–16

Diet, healthy, 221–46. *See also* Foods

Dinges, Dr. David, 215

Distractions, limiting, 119, 144–46, 160–62, 169–71, 176–77

Dopamine
  addictive tendencies and, 130
  behavior disorders and, 32
  brain waves and, 51
  exercise and, 201
  foods and, 235
  moods and, 32
  playful activities and, 182, 190
  pleasure and, 102, 130, 182, 191–93
  sex and, 191–93
  sleep and, 211

Dreaming
  limbic system and, 21
  purpose of, 212–14
  sleep and, 213, 219

Dual coding, 156–59

E

Eating. *See also* Foods
  caloric requirements, 228
  fats, 231–32
  food guide, 225–26
  optimal health and, 245–46
  overachievers and, 238–43
  portion sizes, 227
  quiz on, 222–24
  salt intake, 230–31
  superachievers and, 231–32
  for wealth, 221–46

Einstein, Albert, 24

Electrical impulses, 20, 157

Emotional responses
  controlling, 25–31, 117, 125, 127, 202
  creating, 131
  "emotional cocktail," 49
  generating, 6
  meditation and, 125, 177
  quieting, 140–41
  risk and, 121

Evaluation process, 40–41

Exercise
  benefits of, 197–202
  enjoyable activities, 198–202
  motivation and, 201–2
  quiz on, 196–97
  stress relief and, 197–98
  for wealth, 195–202

Experiences
  for happiness, 12, 17, 94, 182–83
  imagining, 38–41
  responding to, 68, 177

ABOUT THE AUTHORS

Teresa Aubele, PhD received her doctorate in Neuroscience from Stony Brook University. She is currently engaged as a postdoctoral researcher in the Psychology Department at Florida State University. She lives in Tallahassee, FL.

Doug Freeman, JD, LLM provides strategic planning and organizational management advice for business, nonprofit, foundation, and family clients. Until retirement, Mr. Freeman was designated a Certified Specialist in Taxation under the State Bar of California. He lives in Newport Beach, CA.

Lee Hausner, PhD is an internationally recognized clinical psychologist and business consultant. Dr. Hausner co-founded First Foundation Advisors, a consulting group dealing with families involved in a family business and/or high net worth families of wealth. She lives in Los Angeles, CA.

Susan Reynolds is a journalist, author, and founder of Literary Cottage, a literary consulting firm. She and Dr. Aubele are the coauthors of *Train Your Brain to Get Happy* and write a blog entitled "Prime Your Gray Cells" on *www.psychologytoday.com*. She lives in Boston, MA.